Birth of a Self
in Adulthood

DOROTHEA S. MCARTHUR, PH.D.

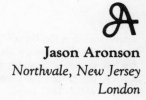

Jason Aronson
Northvale, New Jersey
London

Library of Congress Cataloging-in-Publication Data

McArthur, Dorothea S.
    Birth of a self in adulthood / Dorothea S. McArthur.
      p.   cm.
    Includes bibliographies and index.
    ISBN 0-87668-909-8

    1. Borderline personality disorders.   2. Personality development.
    3. Parent and child.   I. Title.
    [DNLM: 1. Parent–Child Relations.   2. Personality Development.
    3. Personality Disorders – in adulthood.   WM 90 M478b]
    RC569.5.B67M377   1988
616.85′8 – dc19   87–3337
                                                                        CIP

Manufactured in the United States of America.
Jason Aronson Inc. offers books and cassettes.
For information and catalog write to
Jason Aronson Inc., 230 Livingston Street,
Northvale, NJ 07647.

*To my patients for the knowledge
they have imparted to me*

Contents

Psychological Incompleteness of the Parents • How
the Commands Are Communicated • Promised
Rewards for Following the Commands • Siblings'
Differing Responses to Commands • The Myth of
Self-Sufficiency • The Myth of Self-Righteous
Perfection • Misinformation • The Tyranny of Time
and Time as Infinite • The Myth of an Eternal,
Trouble-Free World versus Reality • The Myth of
Compliments • Parental Punishment and
Threatened Abandonment • The Fear of
Engulfment • The Violation of Boundaries •
Patients' Relationships with Siblings

The Difference between Being Needed and Being
Loved • Manifestations of Patients' Anger •
Patients' Concern about Their Parents • Patients'
Temporary Wish to Confront or Abandon the
Parents • Patients Reveal the Parents' History •
Explaining to the Parents • Patients Reconnect with
the Family • Patients Learn to Love and to Build
Their Own Families

Seven Patient Commands
and Their Corresponding Permissions

The Role of Constant Anxiety • Psychosomatic
Symptoms • The Stance or Posture of
Impinged-upon Adults • Relationships with Others
Feel Unequal • Patients' Reevaluation of Their
Relationships • Patients' Confusing Presentation of
Their Capabilities • Patients' Relationships with

Understanding the Patients' Parents • Theoretical
Frames of Reference • Treatment Considerations •
The Borderline Dilemma in Literature and the Arts
• Additional Ways to Study the Borderline Patient
• The Societal Contribution to Borderline
Psychopathology

Foreword

There are many ways in which psychologically disturbed or mentally ill parents can harm their children's lives: they may abandon, physically abuse, sexually misuse, or even kill them. We classify these forms of cruelty as examples of what is termed child abuse, a widespread phenomenon and major problem of contemporary society. Less dramatic are the gross and subtle ways in which parents abuse their children psychologically – in extreme cases in such fashion as to drive them crazy. We have learned that child-abusive parents, whether natural, foster, or adoptive, and whether their abuse is physical or psychological, share in common a particular form of psychological difficulty: they perceive, respond to, and communicate with their offspring as if the children were something or somebody other than who they actually are. We call this *depersonification*; another word for it is *appersonation* (Rinsley 1982). Whatever one calls it, when it operates chronically and repeatedly within a family, it results in serious and long-lasting distortion of the children's developing identity. They grow up unable to be themselves, to function in a healthily autonomous manner, to perceive themselves as separate and distinct from their parents, to perform the functions of the mature adults they were prevented from becoming. Some, like the former movie star Frances Farmer, develop massively debilitating mental illness called psychosis; some manage to escape and grow up healthily—needless to say, we do not see these people in psychotherapy; many—the ones we do see—develop what mental health professionals diagnose as personality disorders.

Many books and scientific articles have been directly or indirectly devoted to the phenomenon and results of depersonification and to the dysfunctional family structures in which it occurs. Dr. McArthur's book is in that genre, but it goes beyond most of them in succinctly and cogently pulling together and explaining the variety of depersonifying messages (*commands*) that disturbed parents, themselves the victims of identity-distorting depersonifications within their own families, direct toward their children. It also goes well beyond Eric Berne's writing on transactional analysis in utilizing psychodynamic concepts to explore in depth the identity issues that form the basis for the confusing "messages" by which depersonifying parents distort their child–victims' evolving self-concepts.

This is, moreover, a book about psychotherapy directed to the literate lay person as well as to the professional therapist, and Dr. McArthur has done a superlative job in producing a text that will appeal to both. Her writing is down-to-earth, her explanations are lucid and devoid of technical jargon, and her clinical examples are invariably relevant and illustrative.

In and between the lines of Dr. McArthur's book emerges the picture of a mature, compassionate, disciplined, and knowledgeable professional whose perspicacity has brought her to a profound awareness of what lies at the root of the problems that bring a majority of disturbed, unhappy persons into psychotherapy. Her book is an excellent exposition of how such a professional, herself mature and hence possessed of the solid identity essential for anyone who proposes to treat others, proceeds to help her patients to understand how their plight came about and how to change it. Furthermore, this book is not an exercise in what has been termed mother- or parent-baiting. Dr. McArthur bears evident compassion not only for her patients but also for their parents, themselves the victims of the distortions they have in turn visited on their children, and she shows how many depersonifying parents may start on the path to psychological health as their children proceed to do so.

Dr. McArthur's book fills an important niche in the psychodynamic literature devoted to personality disorder, family dys-
functionality, and their treatment. It richly deserves, and will
undoubtedly achieve, a wide lay and professional readership.

Donald B. Rinsley, M.D., F.R.S.H.

Senior Faculty Member,
Karl Menninger School of Psychiatry
and Mental Health Sciences

Acknowledgments

I have many people to thank for the creation and completion of this manuscript:

Donald R. Fridley, Ph.D., for his original suggestion that I write this book and his continued support in doing so.

My husband, David, who always supported and encouraged me, giving me the time to write even when it meant reduced time for our family. He insisted that I learn how to use a computer, rescued me from computer accidents, and executed the more complex computer operations to produce the final copy. Without him, this book simply would not be.

My writing assistant, Jane Williams, for her tireless emotional support and constant availability to execute endless numbers of passes through the manuscript to enter new changes.

My patients, who provided me with the information that allowed me to create the "commands" and "myths."

My students, who encouraged and assisted me in creating new ways to explain psychopathological object relations.

My daughter, Miranda, whose birth prompted the creation of the permissions.

Josephine Black, who patiently edited out a thousand extra words and taught me how to write.

Hilary Hanafin, Ph.D., Charlotte Fletcher, Ph.D., Karen

Fritts, Ph.D., and Pam Kensinger, for their critical reading of the manuscript and their support.

Donald B. Rinsley, M.D., F.R.S.H., for his most thoughtful review of the final draft, and his foreword.

My production editor, Elena Le Pera, for her careful and thorough work in shaping this manuscript into its final form.

Dorothea S. McArthur

Introduction

This is a book about adult patients who have been unconsciously held back from traversing the normal process of psychological development. They are not yet separate, whole selves because of their parents' continuing psychological needs. These patients may be unable to complete their education, move into a profession, freely love anyone outside the immediate family, marry, or have children. They have received only superficial permission from their parents to become independent. The main underlying and contradictory message is to stay home and serve as an extension of their parents' lives.

A common diagnosis given to these patients is *borderline*. This term has been used to cover a large number of patients who appear to be neither neurotic nor psychotic, and it seems too general, suggesting that such patients belong neither here nor there.

For the purposes of this book, the term *impinged-upon adults* or *children* seems preferable. This term suggests that those to whom it is applicable have been deprived of the rights and privileges normally enjoyed by a free person. Many impinged-upon adults are talented people, and the word borderline carries the misleading connotation that their physical or intellectual capabilities are only marginal.

People who have had an impinged-upon or otherwise impoverished childhood are often condemned to an incomplete adulthood with compromised satisfaction. A psychotherapy in which the issues are properly understood is one of the few ways to provide a reprieve from this fate.

Feelings about an enmeshed relationship with parents seem to surface at the beginning of each new life stage until the issues are understood. A few patients are fortunate enough to get some psychotherapy during their adolescent years when they are first attempting to break away from home. Most of my patients seek therapy between the ages of 25 and 35 because they see their friends are surpassing them in the life steps of marriage, profession, and procreation. I also see some patients in their 40s or 50s who are looking back during a midlife crisis at the life that seems unsatisfactory or unfulfilling. The longer patients wait, the more severe, impulsive, dramatic, and turbulent are their accumulated feelings. Abrupt changes in profession, marriage partner, and living arrangements often represent an unaided attempt to cope with this problem. With psychotherapy, it is never too late to examine what has happened and why.

This is not a book about teaching patients to dislike their parents. Instead, it is an attempt to help both parents and children understand why they have not been able to continue with life in a productive way. Pathological parental messages are passed on to children with a certain level of deception but in most cases without conscious destructive intent. The parents of these adult patients may have themselves been prevented from becoming whole, separate persons by their parents. Therefore, in each successive generation, the parents have no choice but to send underlying messages to their children for the purpose of enlisting an offspring's lifelong aid in making the parents feel psychologically whole.

The patients' problems are examined in order to pave the way for healthy interaction between patients and parents. A new relationship is possible if both parents and patients wish to make the necessary changes. Parents and patients may become estranged for a time because in the process of understanding and changing, the patients may feel angry and distant. Without the aid of psychotherapy, the parents may also respond to their offspring's changes with psychological and physical abandonment. When psychotherapy is completed, however, the patients' growth and new stance with respect to their parents is often sufficient to ease the long-term tension between them. The patients become able to foster a new relationship that sidesteps psychological difficulty and supports their parents in a healthier way. The patients are then able to go on with life, while their parents are given a chance to function more completely without their offspring as their extension.

This book describes the specific nature of interactions between parents and children that promote healthy psychological growth. In the profession of psychology, the focus has largely been on understanding pathology, and it is easy to lose sight of the kinds of interactions needed for growth.

The material presented in this book comes from fifteen years' experience as a psychotherapist. I originally formulated the concept of unconscious parental messages, or *commands*, to consolidate and organize the similarities in the feelings and experiences of my patients. The commands are used only as a format for responding to patients; they are not directly stated within psychotherapy hours.

The delineation of this therapeutic process begins in Chapter 1 with a number of patients' initial concerns, or presenting problems, which typically appear in the first session. Chapters 2 and 3 describe the underlying commands given unconsciously by mothers and fathers. Each of these "unwritten" rules is contrasted with a growth-producing permission that can replace it. In Chapters 4 and 5 the patients' relationships with their families during treatment and ways to meet the psychological needs of both patients and parents are considered. Chapter 6 explains the ways in which patients pass on commands to peers as a result of their own sense of psychological incompleteness. These commands are also contrasted with corresponding permissions. Chapter 7 explores the way a patient relates to people outside of the family. Chapters 8 and 9 present in detail the patient's relationship with the therapist and the therapeutic issues that need to be addressed to enable the development of a whole, separate self. A review of the literature has been provided in Chapter 10, primarily for the benefit of the mental health professional.

The vignettes included in the text present examples of the commands in the words of the patients. Some of these vignettes represent a compilation of thoughts expressed by many patients, and each has had all identifying information changed or deleted to protect the confidentiality of the patients. In addition, all the patients cited have given signed permission to use brief segments selected from their psychotherapy.

Growing and questioning are especially dangerous tasks for the particular patients described in this book because the underlying messages from the parents oppose them. If impinged-upon adults avoid professional help, they may remain caught in what Roger Gould (1978) described as

> a hostile dependency on those who control our safety because we can't freely see, feel, or act in a way we believe is correct. We can't afford to form judgments that contradict divine [parental] rules. . . . Because we are afraid of our core, we have no access to heightened passions. . . . We can't trust our intuition, so we lose certain nuances in life and impoverish our interpersonal relationships. We can't trust our own assessments of reality, because we constantly need endorsements from someone who is bigger. [p. 42]

After repeatedly encountering their inability to go on with life, at whatever stage, impinged-upon adults feel confused and caught. Gradually they realize the necessity of psychotherapy. This book represents an opportunity to share a therapeutic perspective for working with adults who are seeking to gain the independent lives they deserve as whole, separate people.

The psychotherapy for these patients tends toward the kind of exploration that Bettelheim (1982) believed Freud envisioned when creating psychoanalysis. The patients have two tasks: first, to deal with external living parents who are often physically nearby; and second, to deal with the "intrapsychic" parents, or the parental messages resulting from memories that have been collected throughout a lifetime. This dual approach allows

> the soul to become aware of itself . . . to become more fully human, so that we may no longer be enslaved without knowing it to the dark forces that reside within us. By exploring and understanding the origins and the potency of these forces, we not only become much better able to cope with them but also gain a much deeper and much more compassionate understanding of our fellow man [especially our parents]. [p. 4]

Patients who have been impinged upon often ask whether there are any books that address the particular problems they are facing. This book is intended to address that need. It is also for mental health professionals and people in training to do psychotherapy. Much of the available literature is written in complex theoretical language. This is a more experiential book, sharing concepts derived from working with patients. It is written in the personal language used in the psychotherapy hour with the hope that this style of communication will provide clarity for both psychotherapist and patient.

Many people with whom the information in this book has been shared feel that it speaks to their own lives and the lives of others they know. The borderline dilemma thus appears to be larger than one originally thought—perhaps a pervasive feature of the human condition. This book is intended to encourage solutions toward growth and independence and is based on my belief that therapists, parents, and children can understand enmeshed relationships well enough to realize the birth of a self in adulthood for any person who wishes to take on the challenge.

The commands may be useful to therapists trying to understand their patients and themselves, but therapists must search for the theoretical orientation that best corresponds to their view of life and experience. Some therapists will benefit from seeing patients' issues in this frame of reference; for other therapists, the commands will become a point of departure from which a new, more relevant theory may be created to enhance their individual understanding. This book will hopefully generate useful dialogue, conflict, argument, criticism, and support for the purposes of expanding psychotherapists' understanding of human difficulty with life's course.

Dorothea S. McArthur

CHAPTER 1

Presenting Problems

FIVE PRESENTING STATEMENTS

Impinged-upon adults come into their initial psychotherapy hour with concerns about their failure to manage life. At this point, patients are usually not yet able to speak directly about their problems. The therapist must attend not only to the words but to tone of voice, emphasis, and nonverbal communication. It becomes the therapist's job to understand and then to translate hidden messages. Patients usually experience tremendous relief when the therapist is able to do so, and there is no more effective way to build a solid working alliance. Despite their confusion, patients all present one or more of the following issues:

1. My parents and I are so *close*, but I don't feel that I know them. They have given me so much, but I don't understand why I don't feel given to. I always feel guilty that I have not given enough back to them. I am very angry with them, but I know that I shouldn't be. I don't know why. I am dependent upon them in a strange way when I know I should be grown-up by now.

2. Over and over again, I develop my own life more and more perfectly, and then I bring what I have done home to show my parents. I wonder why they are not interested, and why it doesn't make them love me more. I try again and again, feeling like a failure each time.

1

3. I never experience anger with my parents directly, but I have this strange need to refuse to do the things they most need me to do. That happens even if it is the very thing I should do for me! Why? I find myself too content with this state of affairs even when it is hurting me badly.

4. I just don't have any motivation to pursue the next logical step in my life [i.e., marriage, education, promotion, having children]. I don't understand why I don't feel like bothering.

5. I find myself terribly afraid to do something for me, especially if it is in direct conflict with what my parents need me to do for them. I don't understand my fear.

Experience with patients indicates that there are explicit answers to each of these questions. Therapists need to approach the treatment of each new patient with an overview of the conflict and its resolution, in addition to helping unfold each individual life story with its own unique answers. This overview evolves from understanding the underlying communications that patients receive from their parents.

AN INITIAL PSYCHOTHERAPY HOUR

The following transcript has been created as a composite of many initial evaluations to demonstrate the typical feelings and confusions that might be expressed by patients in the initial hours of psychotherapy. The patient is a bright, shy, and depressed middle-aged female who came into treatment because she was still living at home and unable to accept a university scholarship abroad.

Patient: I wanted to go abroad, but Mother looked at me with that look on her face that I read as "You don't really want to go, do you?" We didn't say anything to each other at all. I became afraid to go because of the feeling that she didn't want me to leave. My friend then called and asked why I had not accepted the scholarship. My mother overheard me tell her on the telephone that it looked like Mother didn't want me to go. Mother interrupted and said in an irritated voice, "What is your problem? If you want to go, then just go."

I was really mad at her for putting that problem back on me. I did not stand up for myself. I just went blank and couldn't respond [double-bind panic]. . . . I would like to be able to go to a university program abroad. The only thing that keeps me from going is my family. I really would love to go. I want some responsibility. I wonder if I'm making a mistake. I'm afraid that I could never come back home if I didn't like it. My parents would be so hurt. When I mentioned the possibility before, my mother cried, "But I don't want you to go." So I decided that I wanted to be where she wanted me to be; I am not sure that's really me talking [false self; see Winnicott 1958, 1965].

Therapist: You seem very anxious about leaving home, when traveling is a normal thing to want to do.

Patient: Yes, because my mother said that I already have a home with them. But I don't feel like their house is my home anymore. I'm afraid to do what I like to do. Maybe I need to stay with my parents. But I know I'm too old to be doing that. I seem to have come to feel that I need them more than I actually do. . . . If something bad happened, would I need them? I can't tell. I know that when I can get away, I am a much happier person. . . . I'm afraid I'd have to leave forever. They said I could come back, but I don't believe them. Why am I so afraid?

Therapist: You seem to be afraid of hurting them and having them reject you.

Patient: This is a chance of a lifetime, but if I go I could never move back home again.

Therapist: Maybe you would feel so fulfilled that you wouldn't need or want to go home.

Patient: I am afraid of knowing what I really want and who I really am, and not needing them.

Therapist: Why?

Patient: The only relationship I have is needing them. I want Mother to need me. I've overneeded her so that she'll love me.

Therapist: You have needed her, more than you really need to, so that she will love you in return. Is she giving you love or is she needing you?

Patient: I feel that she needs me a lot! Anytime someone needs me that much I feel strangled and caught; like I've just got to get away. . . . I don't want Ma to need me *that* badly. I'm thinking about her more than I am thinking about me. Everything I have is going to her . . . almost nothing is going to me.

Therapist: Do you feel loved by your parents?

Patient: I feel close to them, too close; but I don't think that I have ever had love. What a strange thing to say! Can that be true? Don't parents always love their kids?

Therapist: What did you have from your parents instead of love?

Patient: Mother was there in the house physically, but she didn't seem to think about me in terms of what I wanted or needed. Often, it was like there was not a mother that you could talk with. We were close, but I could not talk with her about my feelings. When I was a little girl, I used to sneak into her room and take something of hers like an earring just so I could feel like I was in contact with her while I was in school. At night, I'd sneak one of her nightgowns into bed with me.

Therapist: When she didn't seem close to you, where was she?

Patient: She was off in her own world. Her world is more important than mine. I think that I missed out on something, but maybe I am just pitying myself. I missed out on a dad who was there and took care of things. Ma was the one who was in charge of the kids anyway.

Therapist: Who took the responsibility?

Patient: I guess I helped Ma a lot because I thought that she had all of the responsibility. I always worried a lot about her.

Therapist: Worried that what would happen?

Patient: That if I didn't help her a lot, she would go away and leave us with no one to take care of us.

Therapist: Like your father?

Patient: I think Ma didn't really want him to be there very much. She wanted me to see that she had all of the responsibility. Then I just couldn't leave her.

Therapist: So you took on a lot of worry and responsibility?

Patient: Probably, I felt sorry for her. I can't tell her that I want to leave because she makes me feel as if I am doing something bad. Everything I want to do is bad. The only thing I ever did that she liked was being a figure skater, and that was because she wanted me to do it. I didn't even want to. I wanted to play music. At least I got to listen to music while I was skating.

Therapist: You did what she wanted in an attempt to get some validation for yourself.

Patient: Yeah, whether I wanted to do it or not was immaterial.

Therapist: What do you hope to achieve by moving away?

Patient: I want to be independent and entirely on my own. I want to see what I can do all by myself, to make the choice by myself. I want to go away where no one can decide for me.

Therapist: You look happy when you think about leaving.

Patient: When I was younger, I kept track of what I wanted to do in the back of my mind. It gets hard to keep on doing that. I feel blocked and depressed instead ... sort of hopeless. I feel so used to Mother's criticism. Not a day goes by that she doesn't find something I've done wrong. It's rare that she has something nice to say. I just assume that what I want to do has no place. I'm always in the background, there to take care of someone else. I feel like I've not been what Mother needed. It would be so nice if I could have been something important to her. I've never been able to accomplish anything that made me feel like I stood out. I am a disappointment to her and to myself. There are steps in life that I have not taken. I've never married, I don't have children. I just live at home and go to school, and work as a research assistant.

Therapist: Do you regard your lack of success as entirely your fault?

Patient: Well, my best doesn't seem to have made any impact. I keep trying. Mother tells me that she did her best, and I should acknowledge that; but she won't accept that I also did the best that I could. I am supposed to understand everything about her, while she doesn't seem to need to understand anything about me. She comes into my bathroom and puts on my new nightgown. She can come into my room any time and read my new books.

Therapist: She puts on your new nightgown?

Patient: I come home and she has on my new nightgown and I am not supposed to be mad. If I want to borrow something of hers, that is very bad. She's made a double standard. Ma is the center of the family. If my father wants to say somthing to me, he is supposed to tell her and she will tell me. We are not to talk with each other. I just let all these things happen without a fight [skewed family; see Lidz 1979].

Therapist: Are you afraid of what would happen if you fought back?

Patient: I don't know. . . . I just don't dare. Something is wrong, and I have to understand why these things are happening. She is "the mom," and she did do her best, but I think she didn't do all of her responsibilities. She did only some of them. She keeps saying that I'm not doing mine. I just don't get it.

Therapist: You seem to feel that you have been a real disappointment to her. It must be difficult to leave home when you feel so unsuccessful. Perhaps you are operating under some real misconceptions that we need to clarify. Have you ever considered the possibility that your mother thought you *so* important to her in terms of feeling good about herself that she can't afford to let you leave home? Perhaps she has a need to criticize you as a form of "clipping your wings."

Patient: No, it never occurred to me to think of it that way. But now that you say it, you may well be right. That would explain a lot of things. I'll have to take time to think about that.

DISCUSSION

From this segment of the session fourteen questions emerge.

1. Why can't I accept the scholarship to go abroad?
2. If I left home, could I ever come back?
3. Why I am so afraid to do what I want?
4. Why do I need my parents' approval so much?
5. Why am I giving so much to my mother, and not feeling loved back again?
6. Is there any validity to my feelings, or do I just feel sorry for myself?
7. Why does my father seem so uninvolved?
8. Why do I feel so preoccupied with worry and responsibility toward my family?
9. Why is my mother always so critical of, or negative about, what I want to do?
10. Why do I feel like I have failed her and myself?
11. Why is my mother always right, and I am always wrong?

12. Is it possible that my mother did fail me in some critical way?

13. Why do I get so confused about the difference between what I want to do and what she wants me to do?

14. Why does my mother often tell me one thing but obviously mean another thing or even the opposite?

Another patient described her childhood in a manner that directly addressed her confusion about her core issue.

I had a number of successes that went unrecognized. I did it all to please my parents. They never seemed to notice. I always felt that sinking feeling that the gap was getting wider and wider between us. So instead of deciding what I wanted, I wanted to please. But I doubt my ability to please others the right way. I always question whether I will be able to make it.

After describing the events of her life in which she managed to break away from her family, she sighed, thought for a long time, and then said, "I got out physically, but Ma got inside me and is watching all the time." After listening to a few comments about the probable nature of her problem, she responded with relief, "You've said things that are on the edge of my awareness, but I never allowed myself to think about them. I feel so guilty talking to you."

These confusing thoughts and questions are shared by a whole group of adult patients who are trying to understand why they have not been able to go on with life. Time is passing by while they stand on the outside wondering if they even care. A woman in her mid-30s who wants to marry and have children may feel correctly that her biological clock is running down. A man may feel discouraged about looking for a suitable wife or advancing in his career.

The answers to the questions raised by these patients take the form of *commands* given to impinged-upon adults by their parents as an *underlying form of communication*. One patient defined these commands as "the unwritten rules from the family that eventually drive a person into psychotherapy." Patients are initially unaware of this communication. Yet it is tremendously important and influential, since it hampers their development of a separate, fulfilling life.

Therapists may fail to treat impinged-upon adults in time if they wait until patients come to the feelings themselves without direct guidance and knowledge from the therapists. This kind of waiting can cost patients many precious years. In addition, experience shows that patients will never be able to describe the hidden communication because they have learned that any awareness of it means that they are "crazy." If therapists know about these underlying commands, they will be in a better position to help patients find themselves and move toward the lives they desire more quickly.

The structure of these commands makes it possible to treat patients more quickly and effectively. It helps to organize therapists' conceptual experience and serves as a framework for the interactions, from moment to moment, in the therapy hour. However, patients arrive at an individual sense of their commands by detailing their own experience.

This book details therapeutic questions from an *experiential* perspective. The art of psychotherapy can benefit from the chance to examine the experiences of patients as well as cognitive theoretical perspectives. Experience and theory can both guide therapists within their professional education.

CHAPTER 2

Commands Given to Impinged-upon Adults by Mothers

Impinged-upon adults have received some confusing communications from their parents. I have postulated this information as sets of commands given to patients by their parents: one set from the mother, the other from the father. They are given unconsciously because of the parents' basic psychological need. These parents do not punish or destroy intentionally; more likely, they are passing on unwritten laws that may have been given to them by their parents. Most patients seem to address all the commands. However, each command has varying degrees of strength, depending upon the patients' families.

Sometimes a parent brings a child into the world before having had the chance to become a psychologically whole and separate person. For completeness, such a parent borrows validation by regulating the behavior, actions, or mastery of the child. This vicarious validation enables parents to feel affirmed by their children's actions and to feel successful. The children remain extensions of their parents without any separate boundaries, much as arms and legs are extensions of the body. Patients experience having given up varying degrees of themselves to their parents (Brown 1986, Lidz 1973).

For mothers, this mutually dependent relationship usually works well during infants' natural symbiotic period. However, this system begins to break down as soon as toddlers wish to launch their own lives on a more independent course. To survive psychologically, such mothers need their children to be extensions of themselves and need to be needed by those children. Therefore, they take unconscious steps to sabotage their offsprings' independence. This is why they communicate the commands to their children in subtle, nonverbal ways, that is, by gestures, looks, or tone of voice. Rarely are they given as direct communications. In fact, a command may be hidden within a seemingly healthy verbal communication. The hidden nature of the message is important because if confronted, it allows mothers to deny that any command is being given. A good example of this kind of communication occurs at the very beginning of the transcript cited in Chapter 1:

I wanted to go abroad, but Mother looked at me with that look on her face that I read as "You don't really want to go, do you?" We didn't say anything to each other at all. I became afraid to go because of the feeling that she didn't want me to leave.

At an unconscious level fathers understand that their wives need the kind of psychological support that they are attempting to extract from their children. These fathers generally feel either unable or unwilling to give such support; therefore, they have their own set of commands designed to enlist their children's continuing aid in supporting their wives and maintaining their marriages. They are, thereby, free to go to their employment for long hours, during which they attempt to repair their psychological incompleteness and maintain their self-esteem. Like the maternal commands, the fathers' are indirect and nonverbal.

As all this develops, the children feel increasingly unable to leave home and carry on independent lives. They are confused because the surface communication from the parents makes children feel as if they have all the support in the world from a "very close" family who have "given so much." Patients feel a vague sense of anger and a need to cooperate by sabotaging their own progress toward independence. At the beginning of psychotherapy, they are unaware of the commands or the degree to which they feel impinged upon or co-opted as psychological caretakers.

In this chapter the twelve unwritten rules, or commands, given by mothers experiencing separation–individuation problems are presented. Each command is supported by case examples. Throughout this book, the case material presented is the patients' report of what they remember took place. Actual events may be distorted; however, the therapists' concern ought not to lie with proving or disproving the facts presented within each case history, but rather with working to resolve the associated feelings. The reports (now disguised) represent patients' feelings about experiences that affect their lives in negative ways.

A corresponding healthy permission from mothers is included at the end of the discussion of each command. If these permissions could be given without the contradictory underlying commands, children would have a good start in life. Viewed as a continuum, children who receive *only* commands without any permissions may well become psychotic. Most mothers experiencing separation problems seem to know the permissions by heart, believe them, and give them verbally to their children while simultaneously delivering the commands unconsciously and indirectly. It is this simultaneous, contradictory information that is so psychologically disturbing for impinged-upon adults (the double-bind; see Bateson et al. 1956). Higher-functioning-level impinged-upon adults, closer to being neurotic, may have received the permissions more clearly than the commands, whereas lower-level impinged-upon adults, closer to being psychotic, probably received the commands more strongly than the permissions.

TWELVE MATERNAL COMMANDS AND THEIR CORRESPONDING PERMISSIONS

COMMAND 1

You will not be a whole, separate person but remain a perfect part of myself.

Patients report this command with many different experiences. The patient in Chapter 1 tells us about her underlying message by saying:

Jeanne had to show up for the evening meal each day with her seven siblings. Each sibling had to report to their mother what they did that day and what they planned to do on the next day. "Mother passed out our self-esteem each day, to each sibling," by approving or disapproving of the activities they presented. This patient felt that she had no other source of self-esteem. As Jeanne said, "Mother gave it out. We felt that if we left, we would lose it. Therefore, we always had to return for it and wait for it. We had to tell her everything. There were no secrets."

In despair, Sarah said to her therapist, "I can't try to get myself back because I was never there except as a little piece of her."

When asked to talk about her family, one patient responded simply, "My mother *is* the family."

Clara was expecting her mother to arrive in town for a visit and was anxious because she felt compelled to devote all her time to her mother. I suggested that in the future, she could ask about her mother's plans. She said with surprise, "What did you say? I can't believe that you said that! I would never ask such a question! There is no need to ask such a question because I am supposed to be available as a part of Mother!"

The mothers of such patients maintain control by severely discouraging "being different."

Martha was punished as a child for wanting to have a kind of fruit juice different from her mother's in the morning. People who were "different" were excluded from family vacations and family gatherings; in-laws were different family members; foreign movies were different from American films. All were systematically criticized and excluded.

Calling long distance, Linda had an angry conversation with her mother and set some limits. A few days later Linda received a letter that said, "It is a shame that both of us should lie awake at night feeling upset about our conversation." Linda was not wakeful and upset, but Linda's mother assumed that her daughter, an extension of herself, would feel the same way even though they were separated by a thousand miles.

Before psychotherapy begins, patients have to cope with the commands by themselves. These impinged-upon adults find various ways to articulate their problems and to fight the system.

Cecilia used to chant over and over again to herself, "I am me." The chanting would provide a sense of comfort, but she didn't understand why until she learned that she was attempting to erase her mother's first command. Interestingly, she told her mother and learned that her mother used to do the same thing as a child. It was their best attempt to keep their own separate identities.

Arnold used to imagine a movie, with himself as a character. His life in this movie was all planned out for him. He enjoyed the fantasy because he thought he didn't have to take responsibility for his life at all. However, he also used to enjoy imagining that intermission was a time when no one had control over him.

Impinged-upon adults remain enmeshed with their mothers for many reasons. One is that such patients continue to hope that their mothers will eventually recognize their own needs as separate persons. There is no reason for hope because their mothers give a lot to insure that their children perform in exactly the way they need. The patients confuse this with true giving and feel bad about not liking the gift. For example,

Tanya felt extremely guilty for not liking a mother who "spoiled me rotten and gave me everything I wanted." However, Tanya's mother was actually asking her daughter to be an extension of herself and do all the things that she had wanted to do as a child. As a consequence, Tanya took the violin lessons that her mother had wanted, took dancing and sewing lessons, and ate the fattening foods that her mother baked until she became overweight. She felt showered with gifts, food, ballet shoes, fabrics, and money, but she had no interest in or inclination toward these activities. She hoped that someday something that she wanted would be given to her.

The word *perfect* is important within this command. The concept of perfection will be discussed more fully in Chapter 4. If children fully obey all commands, they are "perfect." If they disobey a command, they feel completely bad and are subject to the psychological threat of banishment. These children have been indoctrinated to believe that their parents are perfect.

Anita had a confrontation with her parents concerning her need to move out of their famly home and live in another city. They said to her, "Up until this moment you were a perfect daughter. You are no longer. If you loved us you would honor our opinion and do what we want you to do."

The experience of trying to be a perfect part of someone else is an extremely demanding task, especially if continued indefinitely. Such patients are always busy and feel as if they must work constantly. One such patient said, "I've never had a vacation!" Many of these patients are overadaptive, overconscientious, and excessively worried about making a mistake. They constantly find new tasks to forestall the inevitable criticism that will come if they try to separate or grow away from their parents. Other patients fight back by being blatantly rebellious or passive-aggressive.

One disadvantage of being unable to view oneself as a separate person occurs when there is an illness within the family. Each family member is overly anxious about catching the illness because no psychological boundary separates them from each other. Patients often feel embarrassed coming into a psychotherapy hour with a cold because they are sure I will catch it. They are surprised that I inquire "Do you feel well enough to do a psychotherapy hour?" instead of becoming fearful of contamination and sending them home.

Many impinged-upon adults have childhood nightmares about snakes. This has been interpreted in the past as sexual-oedipal, but it also appears to be a symbol of patients' enmeshment. Children's experience of being co-opted is frequently accompanied by nightmares about snakes waiting everywhere to trip, bite, or strangle. After such dreams, children are often afraid to get up in the morning, fearing snakes under the bed. Frequently, snake dreams recur during the course of psychotherapy for an adult. Each successive dream details the patient's increasing ability to conquer the snakes.

The corresponding permission given by healthy mothers who have achieved a more separate sense of self is as follows:

PERMISSION 1

You may grow to be a whole, separate person. You must never settle for being only a part of me. Neither of us should expect to be perfect.

This permission comes as a real shock to patients at some point in their psychotherapy. Feeling safe is being an extension of someone else. As one patient put it, "I really thought that nothing could happen to me as long as I was with my mother. It was as if she were magic." Later the same patient said to me, "It really troubles me that I am totally responsible for my own life!"

COMMAND 2

As a part of me, you must not dare to love anyone but me, not even your father. You will not have any emotional or physical need for anyone but me. I will provide all.

Before the advent of systems family therapy, psychotherapy tended to focus more on the mother than on the father. Perhaps this was an accurate reflection of a symbiotic mother's need to have the father in the background rather than merely absent.

The patient in Chapter 1 talks about moving away from home to live with someone else:

"When I mentioned the possibility [of going away] before, my mother cried, "But I don't want you to go." So I decided that I wanted to be where she wanted me to be; I am not sure that's really me talking."

One adult patient had a mother who had died when the patient was thirty. The patient had not married because her mother had told her that you could only love one person at a time. Since she felt that she loved her mother, she assumed that she could not marry until her mother died.

Maria is an unusually attractive and vivacious young woman. During early adolescence, she remembers her mother saying just before she left for her first high school dance, "No man will ever love you because you are not beautiful. Anyway, no one will ever love you as much as I do." Maria already felt discouraged about herself because her mother had blocked her attempts to become a gymnast and a dancer with the phrase "Good girls wouldn't do such things." Maria said, "Whatever hopes I had about being married were severely compromised with these two statements."

Tom developed a relationship with a woman and felt that it was time to make love with her. This was a difficult step for him because his anxiety about having severe asthma would prevent his achieving an erection. When he was able to identify the asthma as a physical expression of disapproval from his mother, he gradually allowed himself the freedom to make love. Many men discover that their anxiety about impotence-related difficulties is the work of an intrapsychic, sabotaging mother.

Patients often say that their parents send Valentine cards to their adult children rather than to each other. The parents may be trying to provide, within the family, what should come from an external romantic relationship. These patients get more disturbed about failing to get a valentine from their parents than about failing to get one from a boyfriend or girlfriend. Parents of enmeshed families tend to celebrate all their wedding anniversaries by asking their children to participate in or plan the celebration for them. The patients show significant progress when they are able to feel resentful at having to plan and participate in their parents' wedding anniversary in place of having their own.

In addition to not feeling free to have relationships with other people outside of the family, impinged-upon adults rarely have pets. Animals are easy to love and are loyal—a kind of loving different from that expressed between parents and their impinged-upon children. Rarely are impinged-upon children able to convince their parents to get a pet. If there is a dog or cat, the children are admonished by the parents not to hug or kiss it because the parents view such affection as "dangerous," "disgusting," or "dirty." It is probable that the parents feel threatened by this affection and move swiftly to attack it.

Don was raised on a farm and wanted to train and ride a particular colt. His mother and father said, "That is something you can only do on your own when you are grown up." He also loved one of the cats but showed his affection to the animal when his father was not in the barn.

If patients from an enmeshed family try to marry, the sabotage can be intricate and complex. Often, the mother succeeds in subverting the relationship and the marriage never takes place. This may be done by encouraging sons or daughters to date other people after the engagement has been announced. If she cannot dissuade her child from the relationship, she may become so overly involved that the couple begins to fight and break apart under the stress of her intrusion.

Dan's mother cried when he announced his intention to have a birthday party for his girlfriend. She said, "I don't believe that you are not going to take care of me." When this strategy failed, she created the party list for her son's party and would repeatedly review the list guessing what his date would be given for birthday presents. In her fantasy she managed to take the place of his girlfriend in opening the presents. The couple argued because of the stress created by the mother's behavior and began to think of the party as a chore.

There are many versions of what happens when patients announce engagement plans. They all report feeling extremely uneasy about breaking the news to their parents but don't understand why. On the surface, the parents may even feign support.

Dan was told that if he found a woman he felt was right for him but whom his parents didn't like, he should marry her anyway. When he actually brought his fiancée home, he faced strong opposition. He reminded his mother of her comment and she stopped speaking to him. Dan's uneasiness prompted him to tell a lot of other people first, to practice and see if he received supportive responses. When his parents learned that they were among the last to hear about the engagement, they were furious.

The patients always hope that their parents will be pleased and supportive. However, the parents seem to come up with one of four responses:

1. Genuine support followed by blatant sabotage.
2. Pretended support that they know they should give which tends to be falsely sweet.

..ootage presented with disturbed emotion.
.. There is no joy and celebration.

contrast, the psychologically healthy permission that
c.. ..ponds to this command is as follows:

PERMISSION 2

As a separate person, you may grow to love your father and then others outside of the family. I am your mother, but you must go forth and meet other people who will provide all that does not rightfully belong within our special relationship.

COMMAND 3

You will not leave me physically or emotionally. If you do, I will withdraw from you. If circumstances part us, you will be in a continuous state of anxious alertness to intuit my psychological needs. You will conduct yourself in ways that validate and calm me (Gardner 1985, Mahler 1975). Any failure in this task will bring a terrible emptiness, anxiety, and guilt.

Mary was somewhat resistant to clarification of her enmeshed family system until she looked at some detailed maps of the resort island of Nantucket, to which her family returned for many summers. Exploring these maps gave her a severe anxiety attack and a feeling of great sadness. She found that although her family had rented a different home each season, each move was no more than a five-minute walk from the previous house. As a child she believed that the move was so far away that it was impossible to return to see the friends she had made the previous summer. She saw on the map the small radius that confined her to her family. She saw missed opportunities and experiences.

Arnold said, "When I leave my mother, she gets mad and acts like the old kind of Christmas tree lights. If you tamper with just one bulb, the whole string of lights goes out."

Doug and Marlene went home for Christmas after they had moved away permanently. They had not been home for several years. They brought presents. Their parents' withdrawal was obvious. They were not thanked for the gifts. The Christmas presents they received were inappropriate, and not the quality of gift given to the members of the family living near home. One gift was deceptively wrapped in a velvet jewelry box. The item inside was a sixty-cent plastic item. Another gift was a present that the mother had bought years ago and "forgotten" to give the daughter. It was out of date. It was difficult for the couple to challenge this subtle behavior because they had been given gifts.

Daniel discovered that if he failed to visit his parents twice a day he experienced a feeling "of agitation." His wife noticed that this feeling vanished as soon as he went over to his parents' home. He thought that he "liked to go home" but gradually recognized his feeling to be one of "need" to be home every day, in the same way that a patient with lung problems needs a new supply of oxygen. As an extension of his parents, he had to get an emotional refueling. The parents had difficulty accepting any reason for his not appearing, no matter how good it was.

Many patients are so afraid of the anxiety and guilt that they might feel if they moved away from their parents' home that they experience a strong wish never to leave. The patients who do move away often feel a flood of anxiety when their parents call or write. They feel compelled to respond to the letter or phone call as soon as it is received, even if it is inconvenient for them.

Therapists often need to raise the question, Who exactly is it that misses whom? Patients experience missing their mothers, but in truth, they have been taught to miss their mothers because the mother feels that she can't manage without her offspring.

Most impinged-upon adults are overly sensitive to other people's feelings, especially in response to their own actions. These disproportionate sensitivities have been developed to detect and respond to parental needs. It is like a beeper, always on alert to detect the necessity of immediate response, even when the mother may be thousands of miles away. This quality is an asset in situations that call for being sensitive to how others feel. However, it can be a liability because patients must block their own feelings to be so aware of the needs of others.

The growth-enhancing correlate is extremely different in its message:

PERMISSION 3

You may go wherever you need to, even though you will eventually leave me. We will both accept our comings and goings as a natural part of our relationship. I will enjoy your departure as a statement of our successful parent-child relationship. I will miss you but will do well without you because I have the remainder of my own separate life goals to fulfill.

COMMAND 4

You will receive gifts from me that I insist you need. They will seem to be a statement of my love, but are actually manipulations to sabotage your mastery and maintain your obligation to me. I must turn aside any gift that you have for me that is also a statement of your mastery and maturity.

Tom commented upon the degree of control that he was experiencing around the issue of giving. He said, "Dad gave me very little, but what he did give seemed to be without a grudge. Mother gave a whole lot, but everything had strings attached. I felt a need to have some control over her gifts because it became overwhelming to watch over all of the strings." For a long time in his therapy, he was suspicious of any gift given to him in the form of verbal support. He feared that I needed him to respond to the support by giving me the gift of being a "good patient."

A grandmother competed with her daughter, Anabelle, for the position of being the primary caretaker of Anabelle's daughter. As a result of psychotherapy, Anabelle began to reclaim her rightful place as mother of the child and wished to take her daughter on an outing. But the grandmother offered the child an expensive, highly desired treat to stay with the grandmother. The child was torn between going with her mother or getting the toy, but decided to stay with the grandmother and received the bribe. Later she admitted that she really wanted to go with her mother but was afraid of alienating her grandmother.

If impinging parents are unable to stop patients from taking a step forward in their life, they may try to stay involved with the patients by offering to pay for the forward step. They may purchase the computer a student needs to do a paper or thesis, or buy a truck for a patient who has decided to become a contractor. Patients need to evaluate such gifts carefully and decide if they really represent support or if they are given in the service of perpetuating dependency.

Sometimes wealthy parents stay overly involved by lending patients a large sum of money. The patients live off the interest, making it unnecessary to be employed. They have been directed by their parents not to spend the principal, so that the money is precluded from use for a growth step. There is no need for a formal contract because patients and parents share the same psychological boundaries. The loan may be recalled at any time, especially if the patients behave independently. The patients feel confused about whom the money belongs to. The money is, in fact, not a gift but an obligation to obey the commands.

Other parents slip money to their adult children. For example, they send a check in the mail without either a request or permission from their offspring. One mother explained this behavior with a note that simply said, "We're sending this money because it makes us feel good."

PERMISSION 4

I will listen to what you want in order to promote your growth. I will give gifts to you out of love and affection. They are yours to accept, reject, or change, and are without obligation to reciprocate. I will gladly accept gifts from you that are a statement of your growth, maturity, and love.

A real gift comes out of observing what children need and then fulfilling this need. If children decide that they no longer wish to use the gift, they should not feel guilty or be punished for laying it aside.

COMMAND 5

We will need and cling to your failures as an affirmation of our dependence upon each other.

The need to fail frequently gets acted out in the therapy.

Charles, a lawyer, flew to another city for an important court appearance. He made an emergency call to me from the airport, to report a number of failures that he felt should warrant the cancellation of his trip. He had had a fight with his mother, had a headache, and had left his child at nursery school crying. He feared that a separation from me and his mother would result in total abandonment. He had provoked these problems to keep himself home. He became angry when I did not encourage him to cancel but instead urged him to move forward in his career as a better way to continue his relationships.

Impinged-upon adults rarely get a chance to feel confidence and pride, since success is usually ignored. Instead they have learned that they get a lot of attention from their families by getting into trouble. Failure keeps family members close together and elicits attention that makes patients feel important and close to the nurturing support they crave. The patients come to understand that consequent parental attention is generally a subtle reinforcement to fail. In this respect, it is worse than no nurturing at all.

Alice suddenly seemed to report more and more failures in her life, emphasizing each failure in a manner that had a manipulative quality. When I questioned her purpose in escalating this behavior, she admitted that this was the only way she knew to request increasing her psychotherapy commitment to twice weekly. I suggested instead that she go ahead with her plan to acquire a job so that she could afford to come twice weekly. She was surprised when I supported this growth step because it would allow her to gain independence from me more rapidly.

Since failure is valued, impinged-upon adults feel awkward accepting and enjoying compliments for a job well done. They expect the compliment to be a disguised demand (see Chapter 4, The Myth of Compliments). They may be deeply embarrassed by any attention to their success. They are skillful at dismissing or contradicting any compliment made by someone outside of the family. This is especially true if the compliment is expressed in front of their parents.

The psychologically healthy permission that corresponds to command 5 is as follows:

PERMISSION 5

We will honor and appreciate your successes as *
growth.

COMMAND 6

You will neither achieve nor master anything unless I specifically
direct it and it enhances my feelings about myself. If you disobey, I will
attack your self-esteem through sharp ridicule of your independent
achievements. Do not fear loss of mastery; I will applaud you for acting
in special ways to enhance me.

Parents of impinged-upon adults are proud of, and openly
laud, their children's talents. What they fail to do is support the
training and discipline that is necessary to develop and utilize
these talents. For example, a mother was overheard saying,
"Look at my beautiful son on the basketball court. He is such a
wonderful athlete; if only he had the training, he would be an
Olympic star." But the training and discipline that would take the
child out of the home and into the real world of competition had
been withheld. Many patients are assured of their talent but are
disappointed that the world does not acknowledge mere potential. As one patient said, "I know that I have talent but no one
helped with the hard work needed to actualize it."

This command is often communicated directly. For example, from the case cited in Chapter 1:

"Everything I want to do is bad. The only thing I ever did that she
liked was being a figure skater, and that was because she wanted me to
do it. I didn't even want to."

Arnold was performing a flute solo. His mother invited many of
her friends to what she called "my concert." Although she was proud of
the performance done by an extension of herself, she was totally unable
to see it as his accomplishment.

Impinging parents can show a systematic lack of support
and can sabotage any celebration of accomplishment throughout
their children's lives.

Matthew and Susan planned their move away from their home-town apartment to their new house. But both sets of parents left on vacation several days before the couple's departure, so that there was no one around to say good-bye and see them off.

Matthew was born with a gift of intelligence that apparently exceeded his parents' capabilities. Each time he mastered a new task, he was given a new problem above his capabilities. He would fail and then be told by his mother, "See, you really aren't so smart." At an early age, he had learned to sabotage himself to preserve his constantly threatened relationship with his family. He was troubled by a recurring nightmare: "I was thrown backwards in space into a black hole. My mother would just stand there. She was getting smaller and smaller until she no longer existed. She never waved good-bye." This dream appeared to represent the power of his mother's sabotage. If he strove to be successful with his superior intellectual capabilities, he would be "thrown backwards" by sabotage. The ultimate threat was to "lose his mother completely."

Graduations are not celebrated by parents of impinged-upon adults because of the feeling of threat implied within this growth step.

Sarah acquired a Ph.D. after her husband had earned his Ph.D. As she left the podium, having received her degree, her father said, "But your school isn't accredited yet, is it?" The letters she and her husband received from their parents were always addressed "Dr. and Mrs. . . .," signaling her parents' and in-laws' inability to recognize her degree. It was hard for her to understand why this was happening. Sarah concluded that she must have failed in some way.

Reacting to her parents' lack of celebration of her graduation, Yolanda went to a florist and got some day-old flowers. She brought them home, made herself a corsage, and put a bouquet of flowers on the kitchen table. Her friends had parties, but there was no celebration for her. She tried to resolve the issue by deciding that she must not have deserved it, even though she had achieved excellent grades.

In contrast, other parents need to acknowledge their children's graduation because it exclusively or primarily serves to prove their value as parents. These families have lavish celebrations with expensive gifts and friends of the parents in attendance. These celebrations have little to do with their offsprings' feelings or needs.

This command is particularly destructive, especially when mothers require their children to achieve to support the mothers' self-esteem. Children sense the command to achieve for their mother and may rebel by refusing. Unfortunately, at the same time, they must sabotage their own need to continue to grow. As one patient said, "I not only fail to do things because I've been sabotaged, I fail to do things because I need to rebel. I never noticed that my actions were also against myself." Since failure is glorified, patients fear that success will bring punishment.

Alice was showing real talent as a singer. She was selected to sing a number of solos at choral concerts. As she sang, panic rose in her as she fantasized someone shooting her in the back from the chorus.

Some adult phobias result from mothers' warnings that are intended to deter children from mastery. Children who are told repeatedly, "Don't go up any steps that aren't completely enclosed because you will probably fall through," may well fear heights and open stairs. Children who are warned, "Don't get on a horse; it will rear and kill you," will often not attempt horseback riding.

If children break this command and become employed, they may feel uneasy about informing their parents. The first question from the parents of impinged-upon adults is whether the job is volunteer. These parents appear displeased when the answer is negative.

Ruth got a new job that paid her well. After several months her mother asked, "How is your little job going? Are you making minimum wage yet?" Ruth responded, "Actually, I'm making over twice minimum wage." Her mother seemed surprised and then said, "Well, nowadays that is not very much money is it?"

This reaction is a typical one. Parents want to imagine that their adult children are earning very little. Perhaps they feel uncomfortable knowing that their offspring are getting money from the outside world, because it decreases the offsprings' dependence on parents.

Many patients manage to move away from home. They cannot understand why their parents frequently find excuses not to visit. Sometimes they agree to come and then cancel at the last minute, after patients may have gotten their house ready or have even arranged a party. If they do come, they prefer to stay with another relative or in a motel. When they enter their child's home, they tend to be either silent or critical. Patients long to have their parents come for a holiday, to see their home, and to take pride in their ability to cook a good meal. When patients can understand that their parents have a difficult time acknowledging the patients' mastery, they can take this form of rejection more calmly and less personally; still there is unhappiness at the loss of family gatherings in the new home.

The more healthy counterpart to this command is as follows:

PERMISSION 6

You may choose to master anything you wish that will help you enhance your self-esteem. You will have my support for whatever you decide to do that will be positive for you.

COMMAND 7

You will see badness in yourself and see it in others who take you away from me. However, you may not express any negative feelings, especially anger, about our relationship. If you disobey, I will swiftly dismiss such feelings. I can be angry with you directly or covertly, by threatening abandonment. We will not discuss it.

The patient in Chapter 1 demonstrates this command:

Patient: I feel so used to Mother's criticism. Not a day goes by that she doesn't find something I've done wrong. It's rare that she has something nice to say. I just assume that what I want to do has no place. I feel like I've not been what Mother needed. It would be so nice if I could have been something important to her. I've never been able to accomplish anything that made me feel like I stood out. I am a disappointment to her and to myself.

Therapist: Do you regard your lack of success as entirely your fault?

Patient: Well, my best doesn't seem to have made any impact. I keep trying. Mother tells me that she did her best, and I should acknowledge that; but she won't accept that I also did the best I could. I am supposed to understand everything about her, while she doesn't seem to need to understand anything about me.

Later, the patient continues.

Patient: I come home and she has my new nightgown on and I am not supposed to be mad. If I want to borrow something of hers, that is very bad. She's made a double standard. . . . Ma is the center of the family.

Another patient said,

I was made to feel that anything that went wrong was my fault. I'm tired of feeling incapable because of my mom.

Marianne felt angry and then deeply anxious when I was about four minutes late for her hour. She was able to express these feelings to me at the beginning of her session and recalled the following incident. At age eight, Marianne went away from home for the first time on a camping trip. She had arranged for her mother to pick her up when the bus returned to town. She sat at the bus station for over an hour and then decided to call home. Her mother answered and gave no explanation for why she had not picked her daughter up. Marianne became angry, and her mother responded by making her wait for another whole hour. While Marianne sat at the bus station, she tried to think out what she had done wrong so that she could apologize. When her mother finally picked her up, they rode home in total silence. Marianne did not understand until fifteen years later in a psychotherapy session that she was being punished for leaving home and then being angry.

These dialogues out of the past help patients to understand themselves. Such patients feel that they must be all bad and that their mothers are all good. It is as if they were not allowed to grow out of the primitive defense of splitting (Grotstein 1981).

This good-bad splitting is a normal defense in early development but should be replaced by more sophisticated defenses, such as repression, as children gain psychological maturity

(Grotstein 1981, Masterson 1976, 1981, Rinsley 1982, Stone 1986). Command 7 maintains the splitting by insisting upon allocating all bad to children and assigning all good to parents. Children are thus prevented from seeing the world from a more reality-oriented perspective in which all persons have their share of good and bad qualities. The children have tried to be good to gain support and approval. Many people dealing with this kind of command are overadaptive, or they are openly angry and rebellious because they know that something is wrong.

Many symbiotic mothers communicate a sense of badness to their children by focusing on a physical defect.

Alison, who was encouraged to eat her mother's fattening pastries each afternoon, was frequently referred to as a "pig." It was difficult for her to believe that she was not overweight. This command is very effective sabotage. People who feel like "pigs" will not go to the beach or to a party because they feel too ugly to be interesting to other people.

Christine spent several hours, before she came for her first appointment, trying to decide what to wear. She was a secretary and a homemaker. She was confused about whether to dress as a "professional" or as a "housewife." She wanted to dress in a professional way but thought that I might see her as "bad" because she would be competing with me. Her mother had undermined her attempts to have a career. Since Christine had transferred these feelings to me, she thought that I would rather have her appear as a housewife. After anxious deliberation, she arrived in jeans to represent the housewife and a suit jacket to represent the professional side of her. Her concern was a serious one. She wanted to present herself in a way that I would not consider her "bad" and so would really help her.

Alice was one of three siblings. Whenever one child did something that their mother didn't like, all three siblings were punished. They were so well conditioned to respond passively that instead of resisting the punishment, they only counted the number of blows each child received. They did manage to establish an elaborate system of standing guard for each other so that they could do some reasonable things without being caught.

Impinged-upon adults have learned to punish themselves for disobeying the commands.

As a child, Matthew got mad at his mother and actually told her off. Afraid of repercussions, he ran inside the house, made himself a snack, grabbed a favorite toy, and banished himself to the garage. He stayed there for a whole day. His mother never came to get him, condoning his behavior by saying nothing.

Command 7 can be suddenly activated when parents perceive that their children are moving away from the family and into a separate, independent life.

Dawn received a ten-page typewritten letter describing all the ways in which her parents felt that she had been bad over the years. The parents requested a meeting with her therapist to explain this "badness."

These patients have learned that their mother can use her anger to swiftly sabotage and control any move toward independence, but no response from the patient is allowed.

One mother used to hit her son periodically when he wanted to stay up late and read books. As she hit him, she would persuade him not to respond by saying, "Take it like a man."

Some of these parents have the habit of attacking unpredictably. The sabotage comes quickly and then is gone, leaving patients unable to mobilize in time to respond. The patients may prepare a delayed reply only to discover that the next conversation with the parents finds them as cheerful as if the attack had never happened. The patients' response is suddenly irrelevant.

Many patients lack the ability to use anger in an assertive, constructive manner. They are embarrassed to find that they have been taught to cry instead, accepting anger and undermining from other people without reacting productively. Such patients usually have a large store of unexpressed anger that erupts over something safe or inanimate. Other patients feel depressed as a defense against anger or have sophisticated means of turning the anger on themselves. They will run red lights or treat themselves poorly in terms of basic physical care. Still others have the presenting complaint of feeling "irritable over little things." They can't understand why, because they are members of "warm, loving, close, and happy families." They seem surprised when I suggest that they have a right to honor those unhappy feelings to find out what is going wrong.

I sometimes give my patients the analogy of a pilot flying a plane. Pilots need to be able to see all of the dials in the cockpit so that they can fly the plane properly. Half of the dials represent the positive feelings a person has, signaling that the plane is flying well, and the other half represent the negative feelings, warning that a correction needs to be made. It seems as if patients have been taught to fly their planes (live their lives) with the portion of the dials representing negative feelings covered up. They cannot see when the needle has gone into a danger zone; it is a wonder that the plane has not crashed.

Patients are surprised that they are entitled to "see all the dials." It is a triumphant moment in a therapy hour when patients are able to get mad at the therapist for the first time, see the resulting changes, and find themselves not punished or abandoned.

PERMISSION 7

You will come to see both good and bad in yourself and in others, including me. In the course of our relationship, I will be angry with you and you will be angry with me because our needs will not always coincide. We can discuss and resolve it.

COMMAND 8

You will give up the life steps of marriage, profession, and children to fulfill your commitment to me. Do not fear disappointment or loss because the overriding importance of our relationship will lead you to believe that you truly do not want to take these steps.

In keeping with command 2, the mothers of impinged-upon adults tend to behave in a way that insures that their children will not even have a strong relationship with their fathers. The fathers often work long hours, so that there is not much opportunity for contact. They may be ineffectual and stay in the background. If they do initiate a relationship, it may be an inappropriate sexual one with a daughter and is usually without the mothers' knowledge or permission. In such cases, the daughters must not only handle the guilt of an inappropriate sexual relationship with their fathers, but must reckon with breaking maternal command 2.

Examples of maternal sabotage of life steps have already been given in connection with previous commands. The parents of impinged-upon adults are often very sophisticated at highlighting a problem so that their children will feel a need to abandon a step forward. Enmeshed parents also capitalize on the natural anxiety that often accompanies these life steps. They can be exceptionally skillful at pretending to be supportive while they are really undermining.

Mothers keep their children at home by presenting life steps as impossible to obtain or unattractive.

Evette was constantly encouraged to marry and repeatedly asked why she had not yet done so. At the same time, she was told that she could only marry someone of the same nationality and religion as her family. She decided that she could never marry because so few men fit those prerequisites.

Lucinda had been promised that if she lived at home and took care of her parents, she would never be lonely. She was tempted to accept this guarantee. However, she found herself incredibly lonely and isolated at home watching her friends go on with their marriages and careers.

Don was taking an advanced qualifying examination in architecture. His parents learned about it and asked, "What happens if you fail?" He was able to respond, "I don't know because I haven't felt a need to read that part of the booklet yet." His answer showed his increasing ability to resist his parents' sabotage and to believe in his ability to succeed. His parents never bothered to find out if he had passed the examination.

PERMISSION 8

You will wish to leave me to accomplish your own life steps of marriage, profession, and children. If you don't, I will confront you.

COMMAND 9

You will never be rid of my psychological need for you to be part of me. You must never grow out of it, because I need continued symbiosis. But I will always reject any offer of intimacy or love. I am not interested in understanding the difference between symbiosis and intimacy.

People seem to be born with a sense of what loving is and an ability to feel when it is not there. Dan said, "I wish that I could have a chance to love my mother without having ropes tied around me." He intuitively knew the difference between loving and enmeshment.

The lack of separateness is a difficult concept to articulate to patients because so much of the pathological communication is covert.

Marianne felt especially "down." Her parents had excluded her from a family financial investment because she deliberated too long before deciding to participate. She was hurt because her sisters were included in the transaction. She felt one sister was her mother's favorite. In reality, this sister was even more deeply enmeshed with her mother. The two sisters had a history of fighting with each other. I shared an analogy with her that seemed to help her understand her feelings. Suppose that her mother was not a whole person, physically, and had asked her to function as part of one of her legs. The "favorite" sister was an even larger part of the other leg, with the two legs competing to win the mother's approval and attention. The mother's rejection of Marianne made her feel like an amputated leg, still dependent upon a body that was no longer available to sustain her. All she could think about was how she could get back into her mother's good graces to reconnect the leg to the body. I suggested that Marianne needed to slowly grow her own new body for the leg. She felt hopeless about accomplishing this task; I agreed that it was difficult but not impossible. She gradually saw the challenge and mastery that lay ahead and developed an interest in the person she was becoming.

Tom called his mother on her birthday. The tone of voice with which his mother responded suggested that she felt validated, reinforced, and therefore wonderful that her son had called. Tom sensed, however, that she did not feel glad to hear from Tom as a person and didn't care about Tom's feelings. Tom said, "I felt like I had done the right thing to maintain the relationship, but I felt no intimacy or real contact. Therefore, I couldn't think of much to say. I was left feeling unfulfilled; our conversation had only benefited my mother."

It is a difficult task to stop being a part of parents. First, patients have to realize that something has been deeply wrong, a dangerous thing to know when one has been so thoroughly indoctrinated by the commands. Then it is necessary to face the difference between loving and needing someone, and the difference between "being given to" and "being used by" someone. Next, patients have to accept the reality of being cared for and desperately needed but probably not loved in the full sense of the word because the parents did not feel psychologically whole enough to participate in a mature relationship. The patients must acknowledge that they are psychologically incomplete. In order to survive and be loved, they must develop the parts of themselves that are missing. They must find out who they are, whole, and completely separate from their parents.

Part of the unfortunate fallout of this command is inexperience with real loving and the inability to receive it from others. Patients feel shy and awkward and look for a quick way to excuse themselves. They feel neither complete nor lovable. They have to learn what love is and to give and accept it.

PERMISSION 9

We will grow out of our early symbiosis with each other. As you mature, we will be two separate people exchanging affection, intimacy, respect, and a mature dependence upon each other. We will be together and apart. Our relationship will always be special but should never preclude intimacy with others.

COMMAND 10

You may not become involved in psychotherapy. Therapists are evil and will tear apart our closeness. What goes on within our family must remain private.

When this concept was suggested to one patient, she said, "My family has always felt that they could provide everything that was needed right within the family better than anyone else." Any expressed need for psychotherapy appears disloyal and implies that the family is not providing perfectly.

This command was amply illustrated by the dream of one patient, Tom, during the initial stages of psychotherapy.

In the dream, I am waiting to see you [the therapist]. You come to the door and tell me that we are going to meet in a different place today. You lead me down a long series of crooked paths until we come to another building. We sit down to start the session. I look up at you and find that your skin has turned to black." I suggested to him that perhaps his dream represented his parent's view that I was leading him down a crooked and evil path. He had to decide in the ensuing weeks whether to believe his parents or his own feelings about the nature of his relationship with me.

If patients participate in psychotherapy that is not helpful, the parents will sense that there is no threat and leave the matter alone. However, if it is a productive psychotherapy, the parents generally feel threatened and attempt to dissuade the patients from continuing. If the patients maintain the therapeutic work, the parents will gradually realize that there is little gained by fighting it. They may decide to say nothing. Should the patients begin to change in a positive direction, the parents will generally articulate the change in a negative manner. For instance, a patient who became able to set some reasonable limits with her parents was labeled "uppity," "self-centered," and "too good for us." However, if patients can fight all the way through to an independent self, parents usually continue the symbiotic relationship by taking pride in the patients' accomplishments because it makes them feel like good parents. By this time, the patients have worked through the anger and are able to interact with their parents in a more understanding way. The parents may even be able to compliment the patients and begin a new relationship with some elements of a friendship.

Parents generally respond negatively to any suggestion that a member of the family having psychological difficulty might benefit from psychotherapy. Often patients are blatantly told, "You don't know what you are talking about." Some parents may even approach the therapist to interfere with patients' psychotherapy. Only a few parents have followed through with an individual psychotherapy contract to make healthy changes in the way they relate to their children.

The healthy correlate of this command permits patients to get help outside of the family without undue embarrassment:

PERMISSION 10

If we are unable to understand and enjoy these permissions, there is something that we have missed. We will seek competent psychotherapy.

COMMAND 11

Neither of us shall come to understand these commands consciously. I must give them to you because they were given to me. If they are disobeyed, you will experience psychosomatic symptoms, strong feelings of guilt or badness, or both. I will convince you that I will die. As a part of me, you then will also die.

The second sentence of this command is the most poignant. Without help, people may be locked into repeating their psychological incompleteness over successive generations. Parents attempt to take from their children what they have not received from their parents and unwittingly contribute to their children's incompleteness. The last sentence usually surfaces during the latter half of psychotherapy for every patient. Most patients report at least one nightmare about their own death, their parents' death, or both. Sometimes parents threaten death very directly.

Arlene had been riding horses for many years on her father's ranch. She decided to buy her own horse. Her mother called the next day to report a very disturbing dream in which both Mother and Arlene were dying of cancer. However, the mother was saved by another sister who brought home a magic medicine.

It was clear that mother had no conscious comprehension of command 11 as the reason for the dream. Arlene felt uneasy about whether this dream might come true until we discussed it in her next psychotherapy hour.

A son managed to leave home and marry after having established a sense of psychological separateness through his psychotherapy. His father responded to this step with a letter that said, "You are like a flower that has been cut off from the plant. You will wither and die."

Patients learn through experience that their mother's statement about death is merely a powerful threat. Parents survive their children's psychological growth, and they benefit by becoming more independent from their children. Many enmeshed parents fill the void left by departing children, finding something new and valuable to do with their lives. Others escalate the severity of the commands to the next sibling down the line.

PERMISSION 11

It is a part of our growth that we both consciously understand the commands or permissions we have been given. If commands were given to me instead of permissions, I am responsible for changing what I pass on to you. Then our own separate growth will be enhanced. We will survive.

There are couples who have worked through the commands with sufficient clarity and understanding to be able to raise children with permissions instead of commands. They promote their children's growth and set limits only on behavior that is destructive to the child or to others.

The following command only occurs in some cases.

COMMAND 12

(To sons; occasionally to daughters) You will be available to satisfy my sexual needs, either explicitly or implicitly. I will ask you not to remember or tell anyone else about this need of mine.

This command appears to be more flagrantly given by fathers to daughters and not rarely results in sexual child abuse. Mothers tend to have a more covert flirtatious relationship with their sons that not only keeps the son from leaving home but causes him a lot of confusion about resolving the oedipal conflict. Mothers tend to invite their sons into the bedroom when they have too few clothes on in the evening, cook breakfast in the kitchen without properly dressing, intrude upon their sons in the bathroom, and rub their backs in a subtly sexual way. The sons become aroused, enjoy the special attention, and frequently settle for being special around the home rather than dating. This issue will be considered more fully in Chapter 9.

PERMISSION 12 (TO A SON)

You will wish to know whether you are a sexually attractive person to me. I will encourge the blossoming of your masculinity and the development of your relationships with other females. I may enjoy your sexuality, but I will never take advantage of you as a sexual person because that has no place within our special relationship.

In conclusion, patients work hard to understand the reasons for the commands. In her attempt to comprehend the psychological needs of her parents, Alice, a perky, beautiful, and insightful school teacher reflected,

You mean that my existence gave my parents a feeling of legitimacy, a feeling that they had a place in the world, and a job to do. I was very special to them for the first few years. When I wanted to do things on my own, I felt like I had lost the specialness. I thought they would be proud, but instead I had become a disappointment, because I was growing out of my need for them.

CHAPTER 3

Commands Given to Impinged-upon Adults by Fathers

The nature of the relationship between impinged-upon adults and their fathers is more difficult to identify than the relationship with their mothers. If therapists have already acquired knowledge about the dynamics of this relationship, they will be better able to detect the subtle clues and ask the questions that elicit information about patients' fathers. On the surface, patients' fathers appear to be in the background. Some fathers have impressive work credentials and are prominent members of their profession and community. They are at their best and most confident at work but feel compelled to devote long hours and many weekends. Even though they may be competent professionally, they still appear to feel psychologically incomplete.

These fathers seem reluctant to demonstrate physical affection with any member of the family, including their wives, and frequently have little to say in family discussions. They will attend important events in their children's lives, such as birthdays, recitals, and graduations, but without enthusiasm. When they step into the foreground, it is because their needs are not being met, or they are trying to keep one of the children from leaving home. Gifts for the children are usually bought by the mothers; the fathers may not even know what the mothers have purchased. In telephone conversations related by patients it is predominantly the mothers who do the talking (skewed family; see Lidz 1973).

As a result of their psychological deficits, both parents unconsciously cooperate to co-opt the separate and individual growth of their children to maintain their own psychological equilibrium. At a conscious level, the parents' actions are always "for the good of the children." The parents appear to believe that their interventions in the lives of their children result from a genuine wish to raise "perfect" children within a "close and loving family." The parents often see themselves as giving up material goods and opportunities so that their children can have experiences they missed. In reality these parents require their children to learn or accomplish something that they themselves may have feared, or been unable, to attempt. For example, some children are required to take the dance or music lessons denied to the mother or father, regardless of whether the children have any interest or natural talent.

Many of the commands from fathers are designed to support the commands from mothers, who are usually the primary parent for the children (marital skew; see Lidz 1973). The fathers satisfy many of their psychological needs at work, and leave the role of taking care of the mothers' psychological needs to their children. Since their marriage may often be unfulfilling, these fathers issue commands that request their children to provide some of what is missing.

These marriages are generally very cemented, in the sense that neither spouse has ever seriously considered divorce. They also tend to be emotionally dry, in that patients rarely report witnessing warmth or genuine affection between the parents. The marriage is more of a partnership based on mutual psychological need than a relationship of loving. These marriages may be dysfunctional but are stable and satisfactorily *ego syntonic* (do not cause internal psychological conflict).

Some marriages are subject to more or less continual fighting, which is accepted and expected by all members of the family with no one knowing how to stop it. In other marriages, there may be a noticeable lack of disagreement. Anger is not manifested by parents or children, with buried resentments surfacing only rarely.

The comments of the patient in Chapter 2 reflect the preceding discussion:

I missed out on a dad who was there and took care of things. Ma was the one that was in charge of the kids anyway. I guess I helped out a lot because I thought that she had all of the responsibility. I always worried a lot about her.

There are eight commands from fathers. Each will be compared with the corresponding, psychologically healthy permission.

EIGHT PATERNAL COMMANDS AND THEIR CORRESPONDING PERMISSIONS

COMMAND 1

You will be with your mother to keep her company. You will do exactly what she needs you to do, so that she can feel psychologically healthy and I can escape my marital relationship by going to work.

Fathers will go to considerable lengths to see that the children stay home with their mother.

A father forbade his daughter, Susan, to walk home from school by herself or with a friend, even though she was a teenager and the neighborhood was reasonably safe. This meant that her mother had to drive her to and from school each day, precluding friends and outside activities after school. Mother and daughter were "put together" each afternoon to prepare dinner and do the housework.

There are many different ways to try to keep offspring at home.

Sam's father took him out to teach him to drive a car. But as soon as Sam made one mistake, he was told, "pull over because the lesson is over for the week." It took a long time to learn to drive that way, although he finally mastered the task. At age 18, he decided to take a trip to see a friend about fifty miles away. He knew that his father would never give him permission to go. So he started out before his parents awoke, leaving a polite note explaining his trip and the time he would return. He received an embarrassing public lecture. All his pride in mastery was gone, and he felt as if he were being led back in chains to his cage. When Sam began therapy, he was driving a broken-down truck that was running too poorly to allow travel on freeways. He had restricted himself to the immediate areas, just as his father had restricted him. Eventually, he worked his way through these memories and feelings enough to buy a new car and take a job that required freeway travel.

Martha planned to take her first vacation away from home with her husband. Both of her parents suspended their daily phone conversations with her for a couple of days before she left on the trip. Her father refused to come for dinner to celebrate his birthday and criticized the present she brought to him. When she returned, her father did not acknowledge the trip and never asked Martha anything about it. Finally, she and her husband were excluded from the next holiday celebration.

Such a reaction from a father can be devastating. Martha needed support for a new growth step and had little understanding of why her father ignored her. In fact, in the absence of understanding, patients usually elect not to venture away. They prefer to stay home and serve the family, even if they do so with resentment.

Sally was home during the summer before she found a condo and moved off on her own. She had a terrible fight with her father shortly before she left home. He felt she had not "discharged her obligations" of doing the laundry in the same way that her mother did. In discussing the matter, Sally referred to some of the laundry as "mother's laundry," which she differentiated from "my own clothes." Her parents were extremely upset that she should need to make the differentiation. The daughter wound up crying hysterically because she "felt crazy." At that time she had no way to understand that her parents were disciplining her for leaving home and that her father was admonishing her for disobeying the first paternal command.

The psychologically healthy counterpart to paternal command 1 is as follows:

PERMISSION 1

You will be symbiotically attached to your mother in the beginning of your life, to meet your and her needs. She will help you to begin to perceive yourself as a separate person. She will provide some manageable delay in meeting your needs so that you can begin to perceive and differentiate between yourself and others. I will be available to help you become separate, explore the world, and come to understand who you are and the positive qualities you have to offer.

This permission recognizes that an initial symbiosis appears to be an essential prerequisite for normal development. It also acknowledges fathers' traditional role in helping mothers and children move toward more separate, individuated relationships (Kaplan 1978, Mahler 1974, Winnicott 1958, 1965).

This particular statement is being replaced in many families by a newer one, which includes fathers in the original symbiosis. Now it is increasingly acceptable for mothers to pursue careers in addition to child rearing, and both parents share in providing even the original symbiosis. When both parents work, they spend more equal time with their child from the beginning of the child's life. Therefore, a more up-to-date permission might read:

NEW PERMISSION 1 (FOR THOSE MEN WHO SHARE PARENTING)

Your mother and I will be with you symbiotically at the very beginning of your life, to acknowledge and meet your needs. We will help you begin to perceive yourself as a separate person by introducing some manageable delays in meeting your needs. You will begin to perceive a difference between yourself and others. We will be available to help you become separate, explore the world, and understand yourself and your positive qualities.

COMMAND 2

You will not have a serious marital or sexual relationship with any other person because your lifelong task is to help me maintain my marriage (rubber fence; see Wynne et al. 1958).

Maria used to watch a woman walk by her home each day to work. This woman had a professional career but had never married, and lived at home with her parents. Maria's father used to say, "See that attractive woman? That is how you can look if you don't get married and have children." Maria is very attractive. For many years, she pondered whether to "lose her attractiveness by getting married."

Donna, a college student, dated a number of men who were unsuitable marriage partners. By limiting herself to this kind of man, she did not have to oppose her father's wishes. Then she fell in love with a first-year medical student and accepted his marriage proposal. She said little to her parents during the beginning of their courtship, but after some time, she became afraid of not sharing her marriage plans. She arranged to see her parents but felt uneasy about the journey home, without understanding why.

When her fiancé formally asked her father for Donna's hand in marriage, the father initially agreed. Then, after a week, he demanded a second meeting with the fiancé. He questioned the young man for a long time. Donna was disturbed, but did not feel separate enough from her father to stop him. Finally, she said, "That is enough, these questions are my responsibility to consider." The couple left the house.

The father decided that his daughter was forbidden to marry until this man had completed his entire medical training, perhaps six years later. Confused and upset, Donna took one of her first steps toward independence by writing a letter to her parents that said, "We have decided to go ahead with the marriage on the date already scheduled. We hope that you will be there." Her parents later were able to participate in the planning of a church wedding ceremony.

Siblings Dan and Mary planned to marry within six months of each other. On the surface the parents appeared accepting, although they shared no part in planning either wedding ceremony. Parental resistance to the weddings appeared to be acted out by another sister who had long been identified as the scapegoat, the "crazy" member of the family. She began acting in a bizarre and sexual manner toward her father. She seemed to be demonstrating that the only sexuality allowed was within the family. This sister threatened to disrupt the wedding ceremonies with "crazy" behavior, which made both siblings question whether a public ceremony was even possible. Dan and Mary were repeatedly called home to arrange psychological help for the sister. When I encouraged both siblings to stop trying to help, and to proceed with the wedding plans, the bizarre behavior disappeared.

These last two examples demonstrate that parents will sabotage their adult children only as long as the children respond by returning to the family. As soon as parents realize that their children will not be deterred, there is usually a decrease in the sabotaging or bizarre behavior. The parents accommodate the new growth step to avoid being left out. At least superficially, they will cooperate with their children's change.

PERMISSION 2

I expect you to leave home and to have a marital relationship. I will support your departure, although I will miss you. I will confront you if you fail to go because I care for you. I will not accept being the only man in your adult life.

COMMAND 3

You will not have any children. Your caretaking needs will be satisfied within my family (rubber fence; see Wynne et al. 1958).

Maria was exploring the issue of whether or not she really wanted to have a baby. At first, she simply felt a preference not to have a child, but felt suspicious of these feelings because many of her friends found the experience so meaningful. Then, she had a nightmare that made her wary of her preference not to have a child. In the dream, she had gone to a hospital where pregnant women went for care. She was dismissed by the nurses because she "did not fit properly on the examining table." She was told to go to the "department of adoptions," a railway crowded with mothers. A train came into the station, filled with infants and young children. The children had a name tag assigning them to one of the awaiting mothers. Everyone received a child but Maria, who was left alone by the track. She woke crying. In considering the dream, she realized for the first time the depth of her wish for a child. It was the effect of command 3 that made her feel incapable of having a child (in the first part of the dream) and not entitled to have a child (in the second part of the dream).

At first, many patients are completely unaware of the *unwritten rule* from both parents about not having children. Initially, they just experience not wanting a child.

Anita explored the issue of whether or not to have a child, even though she was approaching menopause. As she looked back over her life, she said, "Having children has always felt alien to me." I asked, "Did you play with dolls as a child?" She responded, "My parents traveled a lot and always brought me back a doll from the country they visited. They were pretty dolls, but they were put away in a glass case, not to be played with."

Donna and Frank wished to have children but had to confront both an infertility problem and the commands from both sets of parents before they could seriously consider the difficult task of a "special needs" child for adoption. Their own parents reacted to their decision to look for a child by raising many questions about the rights and welfare of the birth parents. The parents seemed able neither to consider the couple's need to have a child nor to assist in the search for a child. Donna and Frank were finally able to locate an older boy. The child lived in their home for many months before the grandparents were able to take an active interest.

There are three reasons why impinged-upon adults may wish to avoid having children.

First, impinged-upon adults discover that they do not feel like whole, separate people who can assume responsibility for the care of another life on top of trying to manage their own psychological growth.

Sally brought a very small teddy bear to one of her psychotherapy sessions and put it out on the table between herself and me. She was actively struggling with the issue of whether to have children. She said, "I carry this with me to remind me that I exist. But at the moment, I feel so tiny." I asked whether she felt smaller than a baby. She answered, "Yes. No wonder I have difficulty thinking about being a mother! As I feel bigger and bigger I suppose that I can buy a bigger and bigger teddy bear. Maybe someday I'll get big enough to have a baby!"

Talented impinged-upon women with a profession already established may feel overly sensitive to further interruptions from work, even the natural ones of childbearing. They perceive menstrual periods, pregnancy, labor, birth, and the care of children transferentially as a sabotaging process imposed upon them by nature and society without their permission. They feel like resisting and find it difficult to see beyond to the joys of loving a child.

Second, it takes time to perceive the difference between the pathological caretaking impinged-upon adults have been giving to their parents, and the healthy support and care given to their own children. Patients have to be introduced to experiences of healthy nurturing.

Third, many patients have already had parenting experiences caring for younger siblings and are "worn out." They prefer to postpone indefinitely the experience of having children, to take care of their own independency needs, giving precedence to other life goals. Sometimes it becomes too late. Then a compromise solution may suffice, such as foster care, adoption, or taking care of a niece or a nephew who may be having difficulty with her or his own family.

The struggle surrounding parenthood is clear from this discussion. Resolution of command 3 requires a great deal of work.

It is gratifying to watch patients move from totally ignoring children to noticing, and then paying attention to, their own need to be parents. When they have their own child, it is a dual celebration. The birth of a baby announces the birth of the psychological self in each parent. Some patients have written later, enclosing pictures of children, saying that they can hardly remember their strong need not to have a child.

If impinged-upon adults become parents, they may find that their baby helps build a new relationship with the grandparents. The grandparents may relate to the grandchild without the psychological commands that they gave to their own children, leaving the impinged-upon adults surprised, pleased, and baffled by this more healthy communication.

If impinged-upon adults raise children, it becomes easier for them to see all the good parts of parenting that their parents were able to provide, in spite of the enmeshed relationship. Patients can experience firsthand and appreciate the number of diapers changed, the expenses, the trips to the doctor provided, and the many different educational and cultural opportunities made available to them as children. These impinged-upon adults may also see, in their own children, their parents' talents and creativity passed from generation to generation.

PERMISSION 3

You may have children of your own and experience the joys and difficulties of parenting. You will reexperience the parenting that your mother and I gave you. Your evaluation of what we did with you is part of deciding how you will parent your child.

This permission shows an important departure from the pathological command in that it allows children to evaluate, and be critical of, the parenting they received. It recognizes that parenting is a difficult, imperfect process.

COMMAND 4

You will not have any profession because your work is solely to maintain my family. If you try to succeed in outside work, I will ridicule, degrade, and minimize the intellectual development you achieve. I will rarely consult with you seriously or acknowledge your expertise.

The sabotage that teaches a child that she has little intellectual ability can begin at an early age.

Ana was an exceptionally bright five-year-old. Her brother, aged six, had an intellectual ability that was average. One day their father was playing blocks with them. He placed a block on a rung of a ladder above their heads and urged the two siblings to compete to see who could retrieve it the fastest. Ana started looking for an object to use to dislodge it, while her brother ran over and shook the ladder hard enough to knock the block off. The father retold this story many times to the extended family, as well as to strangers, allegedly to show how differently his two children approached problem solving. He told the story in front of Ana but said nothing when her brother was present. He seemed to need to lower Ana's self-esteem by pointing out that she could not deal with practical tasks.

Humiliated, Ana wondered if her father was aware of her feelings. She asked me, "How could a father do something like that?" In time, she came to understand that possibly he was threatened by her intellectual potential and unconsciously used this example to make her believe that she was less intelligent than her brother. Unfortunately, he succeeded.

Ronald was given an IQ test and found to be extremely bright. He was told by his father that he was "not normal." Furthermore, since he had this "unusual lack of normality," he would only be allowed "one chance" to master anything. If he didn't get it right the first time, he would have to discontinue the activity.

Alan, a talented professional musician, came to me with the presenting problem of severe anxiety attacks when he practiced his musical instrument. His father would attend most of the concerts in which Alan performed but was reported to have behaved in a "disruptive manner" during the performances.

Alan began to understand the sabotage in command 4 when he reported that he had difficulty practicing because he was sleeping poorly at night. He slept in a position that made his arms go to sleep, and he awoke in pain. I inquired how he slept; it was the position in which he played his musical instrument. He claimed it was the only way he could sleep. I suggested that he was probably attempting to maintain his musical profession while he slept, fearing it might be taken away. This interpretation allowed him some relief and relaxation, so that he was able to sleep without pain and practice more during the day.

Alice came to me with an unusual habit. She found it puzzling that she kept all kinds of scraps of paper, receipts, and small paper bags. These items were piled neatly upon her desk and then stored in her summer home. Family members periodically tried to throw away these "mementos." Alice resisted, with strong feelings, but had no idea why. When questioned further about the nature of these "valuables," Alice revealed that she wanted to be a poet but had felt criticized by her father, apparently himself a frustrated artist. As a result she was afraid to publicly use her poetic talent. She had internalized his command 4 and was unaware that she had devised a way to be an "invisible poet" under the guise of a messy homemaker. Each piece of paper that she collected reminded her of an event in which she had observed people interacting. These situations held special meaning for her as potential material for her poetry, so she had found a way to record each event without ever writing it down. The piles of paper on her desk made her feel secretly creative while she maintained tremendous resistance to writing anything down. I suggested that she sort through the pieces of paper and begin to log in a journal a brief statement of each incident. After she had begun this task, she recognized that each incident represented important feelings and needs of her own that had "gone underground" many years ago.

The question whether parents are able to support their children in academic or creative pursuits can be an extremely confusing one for patients. This is because the parents frequently do support good grades. They may need their children to succeed academically or creatively, not for the children's sake, but so that they can feel like successful parents. However, the children sense that there are fragile limits to this support. If the children go beyond what their parents want them to accomplish, into the realm that represents individuation and success away from home, the support is abruptly withdrawn.

PERMISSION 4

You will develop your own mastery within the work or profession of your choice. I will learn and benefit from your experience and consult you if I need your advice.

It is gratifying to be able to grow up, leave home, and find a fulfilling profession. It is even more gratifying to be able to use one's acquired skills to help one's parents, if they need it in their later years. Sons or daughters who become doctors, for example, feel a special pleasure referring their parents to a competent colleague for a medical problem. It is one of the best ways to compensate parents for all the care they have provided over the years. Parents who have difficulty allowing their offspring to separate from them are sadly unable to accept this kind of help from their children.

COMMAND 5

You may not give me any gift that displays your independence, mastery, and maturity. I will not accept it.

John was a photographer who felt guilty about moving away from home. In an attempt to help his parents feel better about his absence, he photographed himself and gave the portrait to them to keep. They took it without comment. Several days later, his father gave it back to him, angry and tearful: "I have no use for such a thing!" He added, "We might have kept it if it had been a portrait of your mother!"

Clearly, his father could only see the portrait as a reminder of John's ceasing to be a mere extension of his mother. Therefore, his father could not enjoy or be proud of it.

Amanda, a patient in her mid-30s, had been unemployed for three years. She had contented herself with homemaking and helping with her family's investments. As her psychotherapy proceeded, she began to rediscover some of her talents. She played a flute solo for a family wedding and created some floral arrangements from flowers grown in her own garden. Proudly she gave a flower arrangement to her father on his birthday. She was hurt that her father could not acknowledge the flowers or the music that she had played at the wedding. As a part of the working through of her feelings, she brought some of her dried flower arrangements into her psychotherapy hour. She expected a negative or critical response from me. It became clear to me as a result of this incident, how deep the scars of sabotage can reach. She eventually created a special flower arrangement for my office that delicately captured all the colors in the decor. It took time for Amanda to absorb my genuine acceptance of this important test of my approval of her need to grow.

It would have been damaging for me to take the traditional psychoanalytic stance of interpreting the gift but not accepting it. Amanda would have experienced such a stance as further sabotage. It was not only a step forward in terms of her artistic growth but was also a nonverbal statement of her emerging trust in her relationship with me. One of the tragedies and joys of clinical work is to discover the variety of talents long hidden in patients.

Many impinged-upon adults show shyness and embarrassment at the prospect of sharing their creative work with someone.

Arlene, a singer, had recently attended an excellent series of workshops and done well as a participant. She wanted to mention the workshop and her experience to me since she had learned that I was also a singer, but felt afraid. She feared that I would belittle and reject this information by saying "Didn't you know that I have already taken such a workshop and done very well" or "Don't you think it is presumptuous for you to think that I didn't know about that." Actually, I was touched by the caring and thoughtfulness implied in this communication and thanked her for the useful information. The response she had feared was command 5.

PERMISSION 5

You can give me gifts that show your developing maturity, independence, and mastery. I will enjoy them, although they may also bring some sadness as you move away from needing my parenting.

COMMAND 6

You will obey your mother's wishes without question or anger. I will support her in any attitude or action by which she may use you to maintain her psychological equilibrium. I will not consider your feelings.

If children fail to meet their mothers' needs, fathers will often step out of their customary role on the sidelines to participate in admonishing their children. Sometimes fathers have difficulty understanding what the mother is doing, but they will still follow her lead and agree with everything she says.

Adult patients from enmeshed families become accustomed to ritualized family lectures that follow the same format. These "family discussions" are often deceptive because they appear to be held in an atmosphere of friendliness and warmth. Patients are invited for dinner or dessert. Then the atmosphere changes; demands and criticism begin. It is frequently impossible to fight back because a logical argument will not succeed, and the patients' feelings don't count. As one patient said, "Arguing with Mother is like walking into quicksand. There is no way out." Another patient said, "When Mother's insecurities are present, there is no place for mine." These discussions can be psychologically painful. Patients, feeling the tremendous power of both mother and father, quickly lose any sense of themselves. This loss of self can feel painfully like psychological death.

These encounters tend to have tremendous impact. The "real self" (Winnicott 1958, 1965) usually goes into hiding, whereas a "dazed child" tries to comply so that the situation will end as soon as possible. The purpose of these parental lectures is to establish limits on what the offspring is permitted to do with his or her own life. To the impinged-upon children, the lectures seem unreasonable or nonsensical. The lectures will not stop until the children demonstrate compliance, usually by crying. Then the children can be embraced by mother and father and told, "It was all for your own good."

Some patients have experienced periods of hysterical crying after such a confrontation, but with no real sense of what was happening. Sometimes, the crying is delayed for years and surfaces in a psychotherapy hour. Once patients have worked through the feelings associated with these confrontations, they become better able to detect the signs of their recurrence and can refuse to participate.

PERMISSION 6

If a family member, including your mother, asks you to do something that is not good for you, please let me know, and we will discuss it until it is satisfactorily resolved.

COMMAND 7

If you disobey these commands, I will disapprove and will tell our friends that you are ungrateful, unloving, and uncaring. If you obey, I will ignore you with my continual absence. I can never love you as a whole person or care about what you try to give me, because I have to sacrifice you as an appendage of my marriage.

Patients will face this unwritten rule anytime they feel a need to disobey the commands or confront their parents. For several reasons patients usually wish to do this at some point during psychotherapy. They have learned that they can and must free themselves; they are angry and wish to say so. As patients begin to feel stronger and more separate, they want to assert themselves and see if they can "win" for the first time in their life.

As a therapist, it is advisable to halt this kind of confrontation for two reasons: First, the parents are unprepared for a fight and will not be able to oblige the patients. Second, the parents cannot possibly understand the dynamics any better than the patients did before therapy. It also seems that the patients' anger is more satisfactorily worked through with the therapist in the privacy of the consulting room. Patients who stage such confrontations without the therapist's knowledge usually regret the outburst later because of its destructive consequences for the parents.

Despite the therapists' warnings, confrontations do occur, provoked by patients, or brought on by parents because they notice changes in the patients. It is during these altercations that the first part of this command is given by fathers in a desperate attempt to bring patients back under the control of the enmeshed family system.

Don fought with his parents because he had failed to do what they recommended in terms of buying a car for himself and his two children. His father told him that if he disagreed with them, it meant he did not feel love or respect for his parents. He was no longer their "perfect little boy"; in fact, he had become "hard as nails" and "cold" since consulting a therapist. They also attacked his profession and his ability to be an adequate husband. Finally, they rejected him by slamming the door in his face. He handled the confrontation quietly, and although deeply disturbed, he was able to hold his ground. When his parents saw that he did not change his mind, they phoned him the next day and tearfully offered to take him out to breakfast.

As a result of this argument Don began to examine the following questions with me. "Do I love my parents?" and "Do they love me?"

Definitions of love vary widely. Command 7 suggests that some fathers are not able to love their offspring as whole, separate persons. Many therapists would say that loving is present in addition to the commands, but love occurs as part of the permissions, not as part of the commands. The ability to love has two prerequisites: feeling like a whole, separate person and being able to value and take good care of oneself. Love requires intimacy, but incomplete people do not dare to risk sharing themselves intimately with anyone. Therefore, most of the interactions described in this book cannot be regarded as *loving*.

Instead, they are more properly viewed as arising from *psychological need*. The difference between psychological need and love will be discussed more fully in Chapter 5.

Many daughters go to great lengths to get love from a father, even though he repeatedly demonstrates his inability to give it.

Mary described an incident from childhood in which she sprained a wrist on a water-skiing expedition. She showed the wrist to her father, a surgeon, hoping to receive some of the tender medical care he gave easily to his patients. He said that he thought the wrist was not broken but that she should hold it upright to decrease the swelling. She went to bed that night and kept herself sleeping lightly to hold the wrist down so it would swell more! She was hoping to accomplish two things: one, to get a few days relief from mandatory violin lessons which she hated; and the other, to get a trip to the hospital with her father for an X-ray. She got the trip to the hospital, but her father misread the X-ray. This kind of manipulative behavior was painful for her to admit and did not generate the caring response she wished from her father.

PERMISSION 7

If we as a family are not able to follow these permissions, we will consult a psychotherapist or other mature helper to find out whether we are sabotaging your growth. If we can use these permissions, we can grow to love each other deeply as separate, whole persons within the boundaries of our special father–child relationship.

COMMAND 8 (TO DAUGHTERS)

You will be available to satisfy my sexual needs, either explicitly or implicitly. I will ask you not to remember or tell anyone else about this need of mine.

This command is given by some disturbed fathers, usually when the marital sexual relationship is poor. The parents may sleep in separate beds or even in separate bedrooms. There is always a good reason for this, such as differing sleeping habits or snoring, but that is usually an excuse to cover an empty relationship. The fathers' remaining sexual energy often expresses itself with their daughters, while the mothers may turn to their sons.

The results are various degrees of child sexual abuse. This kind of violation of physical boundaries occurs for children as young as infants and may continue all the way into adulthood. Even if the sexual contact stops, flirtation and sexual innuendos may continue. Most of the time, children are threatened with harm if they tell. The offspring are powerless to defend themselves because they are not yet strong enough persons to resist. Simultaneously they crave intimacy. Sexual stimulation may well be mistaken for love; children may settle for sexual contact as the best substitute available. Children hope they might get the intimacy they want by cooperating with their parent's sexual demands. The children feel both flattered and degraded.

As the children reach maturity, the sexual acting out that once took place may be revealed by the parents' lack of response to their offsprings' intimate partners. These parents tend to abruptly leave a gathering when the date arrives and to experience difficulty facing their son's or daughter's plans for marriage.

The actual memories and consequent feelings of humiliation, guilt, and sexual confusion may be difficult for patients to retrieve. This is because patients have a deeply ingrained habit of protecting their parents, or the sexual abuse may have occurred at an age prior to clear memory. Instead of the actual memory, patients may have anxiety attacks, psychosomatic symptoms, or unusual reactions or dreams in relation to the subject of sexual child abuse, or they may experience a heightened sensitivity or dislike to certain sounds, smells, or colors. These symptoms and reactions may be the sole clues that sexual abuse occurred. If the sexual abuse occurred when the children were older, there will usually be a clear memory to bring out of repression.

Fortunately, feelings tend to emerge separately, so that they can be dealt with one at a time. Initially patients will experience the feelings of detachment and depersonalization that as children they utilized to survive the experience. Then comes shock and disbelief that sexual experience actually happened, coupled with fear of death about revealing the truth. Then rage, feelings of betrayal, a strong urge to rebel at the intrusion, and a desire to retaliate emerge. There is shame, helplessness, despair, and feelings of inadequacy that they allowed themselves to be sexually abused, and guilt over any physiological pleasure or arousal that may have resulted from the experience. The patients reexperience feeling sad and alone because no one was around to stop the problem.

If the father acquires the sense that he is doing something wrong, he will often cease the sexual acting out abruptly, leaving both parties in a state of arousal and psychological incompleteness. The child may wonder if the parent suddenly withdrew because the child was not sexually attractive or was inadequate in some respect.

Negative feelings about sexually abusing parents will often be transferred to the therapist. In this case, patients will see the therapist as violating their boundaries by merely suggesting that the patients talk about sexual abuse. The therapist becomes a person who tells the patients to do things that are not good for them. Therefore, the therapist cannot be trusted.

This difficult area needs to be worked through as much as patients can allow, in order for them to be freed from ambivalence and to become fully sexual persons. The following permission helps children to feel sexually adequate.

PERMISSION 8 (TO DAUGHTERS)

You will wish to know whether or not you are a sexually attractive person to me. I will encourage the blossoming of your femininity and the development of your relationships with other males. I may enjoy your sexuality, but I will never take sexual advantage of you because that has no place within our special relationship.

Therapists need to be knowledgeable about these commands because the patients' parents will never be able to verify them (double-bind; see Bateson et al. 1956). It is frustrating for patients to be unable to talk with their parents about this problem. If they try, the point will be skillfully avoided. At best, it may be briefly considered in an apologetic manner. It is as impossible to discuss the matter as it is to ask the right arm to cut off the left leg.

The symbiosis and the enmeshment, if not interrupted by insight, will continue with neither person aware of the commands in operation. As one of my patients reminded me in his termination hour, "The underlying rules of my family are a matter of course for me now, but I found them extremely difficult to acknowledge for a long time, partly because they are so powerful."

CHAPTER 4

The Patient's Relationship to the Family

In this chapter we will consider some of the complex ways in which symbiotic families remain as a unit longer than is beneficial for the individual growth of each member. These interactions cause troubling feelings of confusion, guilt, despair, and helplessness for children.

THE PARENTS AS COMPETENT MEMBERS OF THEIR COMMUNITY

Some impinged-upon adults observe their parents as highly valued and admired for competent work within the community. The parents may be intelligent or exceptionally talented and pass their genes on to their creative children. Many parents have managed professional success as another means of healing psychological incompleteness. For example, children may observe the father being elected by the community to serve on prestigious boards or serving as a well-known executive in his field. The mother may be a successful lawyer, a recognized teacher, or a famous entertainer. Parents wield the commands with the same strength with which they make an effective contribution to their profession.

People come to the children and say, "Your mother (father) is such a wonderful person; she (he) does so many things for other people and never takes any credit for it. She (he) must be a wonderful parent to you." The children, observing all this, wonder why they don't feel the same way the community does about the parent. Something must be wrong or "crazy" since they do not perceive the parent in the home as wonderful, supportive, or full of energy and giving. Instead, the children see the parents as somehow self-centered, fragile, and needy.

Why do these talented parents present themselves within the family as fragile and in need of help? Why do they not gain enough strength and sense of value from their work? They probably do, but for them the feeling of value is temporary. It must be renewed constantly because there is not a complete self to contain the experiences of mastery. The community reaps the benefits of their on-going need to work hard. Despite their accomplishments, these parents still turn to their families for their sense of wholeness (Masterson 1981, Rinsley 1982).

When considering the pathological interactions within families, it is possible for patients and therapists to lose sight of the professional strengths of the parents. Once the patients are able to see both sides of their parents clearly, they may be able to support, nurture, respect, and enjoy this competent professional side. Then the patients will be able to help their parents strengthen their fragile selves rather than consorting with and rescuing them, which only continues the psychological incompleteness.

PARENTS WHO LANGUISH

Less frequently, the pendulum swings in the opposite direction. Instead of being competent out in the community, parents may present themselves as severely psychologically disturbed. Assuming the role of the totally incompetent member of the family, they lose their job, stay home, complain, and become withdrawn, physically ill, or even immobile. The other parent remains dominant, manages everything, and complains bitterly about the poor health of the spouse. It is interesting to note that the disturbed or ill parents' health varies considerably and seems to worsen suddenly when their children approach or accomplish a growth step (withdrawing object relations unit; see Masterson 1976, Rinsley 1982). The stage is set for one or all of the offspring to come running back, interrupting, or abandoning the new direction of their life. The parents continue to request outside medical or psychiatric help; but, when it is arranged, they find an excuse not to use it. Instead, improvement in health occurs only with attention from the children. The parents get reinforcement for being ill, which sets the stage for another cycle of disturbed behavior. It is indeed a tragic situation when parents decide to sacrifice any kind of meaningful life to maintain enmeshed ties within the family.

At the same time, the martyred spouses play the innocent victim, with little awareness that they perpetuate their marriage partner's incapability. They need the ill spouse to be "in trouble" so that they can call the children home. The marriage becomes "terrible," but neither parent would ever think of a separation. The children are labeled "selfish" and "uncaring" and feel guilty if they stop attempting to rescue their mother and father.

However, patients can learn to understand these manipulations enough to continue with their own growth steps. They start nonverbally reinforcing their parents' capable behavior and set up situations that encourage their parents to manage on their own. As a consequence, the behavior of the parents often improves.

THE PARENTS IN THE PSYCHOTHERAPY HOUR

Sometimes, therapists get a chance to meet their patients' parents. These parents are proper, usually well dressed, and polite. They want the therapist to understand that their child was very much loved and that they have worked hard to provide life's good things for that child. They don't feel that anything has gone wrong; however, if their child feels that something is amiss, they are anxious to help. They have come into the office to fix the child, not to look at themselves. They prefer to believe that most psychological problems have an organic basis, for which nothing can be done. This strongly held belief is based upon the fact that the child did well during one phase of development; therefore, they have ruled out any environmental influence. They want the therapist to know that their relationship with their child has always been a very "close" one (pseudomutuality; see Wynne et al. 1958). They are concerned that something has happened to that "closeness." They may speak of their offspring's recent disloyalty, if therapy has already begun and the patient is beginning to pull away from the enmeshed family.

On the surface, everything looks fine. The parents seem to know many of the permissions and will swiftly tell the therapist that their child was raised with only healthy messages. They are unaware of any commands or of the psychological need for them. (It is easy for inexperienced therapists to be deceived at this juncture.) Looking more deeply, the therapist will often perceive a brittle and uneasy calm. The parents watch the therapist carefully and may be swayed by his or her reactions. Underneath this niceness comes a communication of a different nature. The patient and the therapist sense unexpressed negative feelings as well as a vague sense of danger.

The patient is obviously tense and looks to the therapist for courage. There is a sense that the conversation could abruptly take an ugly turn. Everyone is careful. It feels as if the parents are not fully there. They continue to maintain that the problem lies with the patient. Everyone is cautious about approaching the hidden or real parents because that might precipitate a sudden, angry departure. Underneath this facade are fragile parents in need of gentle communication no matter what is presented. Any recommendation to understand the psychological functioning within the family is politely refused by the parents.

After the interview is over, the parents may assure the patient that the therapist is a good one. However, they will find a way to subtly discredit everything that was said in the session. The therapist and the patient will probably never know how the parents really felt about the interaction. Parents of impinged-upon adult patients are generally too accommodated to their own incomplete lives to be interested in the kind of help a therapist has to offer. Instead they will act, in effect, as if the interview never took place.

THE PSYCHOLOGICAL INCOMPLETENESS OF THE PARENTS

As patients begin to understand the degree to which they have been co-opted, they demand to know why and how their parents could behave in such a way toward their own child. They feel angry, despairing, and abused, while at the same time protective of their parents. They want to know if other parents have done the same thing to their children.

In answering these difficult questions, it is helpful to address the fact that the patients' parents must also be impinged-upon adults who have likely failed in achieving their own independence and mastery. The phrase "psychologically incomplete" seems to capture the essence of the parents' problems. For a time the patients are barely able to hear this; all they feel is anger and hurt. When those feelings have been released, the patients begin to remember what they know about their parents' own history. Sure enough, it is every bit as difficult as their own. They are relieved to find out that their parents are not "crazy," "purposely destructive," or "sociopathic." They may be deceptive, manipulative, hysterical, clinging, or demanding, but these manifestations are in the service of surviving psychologically. The patients were innocent victims until they learned the rules of the game and became unwittingly compliant participants in their parents' pathology.

HOW THE COMMANDS ARE COMMUNICATED

As was suggested in Chapter 2, most of the time the commands are communicated nonverbally. The following analogy sometimes helps patients understand the nature and power of nonverbal communication.

A mother sits in a rocking chair on the porch with her fourteen-month-old baby. The mother is rocking and looks happy and content. The child sees green grass in the front yard and a red and yellow toy truck on the walkway. He wants to go to the truck. He gets down off his mother's lap and begins to edge toward the truck with anticipation. At the same time, he notices that his mother is beginning to look restless and agitated. The farther he moves away toward the truck, the more agitated his mother becomes. She stops rocking and looks tense. If he turns around and walks back toward her, he notices that she becomes relaxed again. What is this child going to do about getting to the truck?

Impinged-upon adults always confirm immediately their childhood feelings of confusion.

Alex said, "When I go out of town, my mother doesn't say anything, but she slumps in her chair and looks pathetic. I keep having the feeling that she sits in the same position until I return."

Dan's father develops a hearing problem every time his children stray away. One day, he came into my office with Dan and his wife. He dragged a chair all the way across the room to sit right next to me so that he could hear. Interestingly enough, he heard the next patient letting himself quietly into the waiting room. The only things he did not hear during our session were words he did not want to listen to. His hearing problem was apparently a nonverbal communication directing his sons to stay home and mediate his communication with his wife.

Other parents of impinged-upon adults make a strong statement to their children in the form of storytelling. One patient was told the following story over and over again when he was a toddler. "

"You know that you are really not our first-born child. Before you, we had a little girl named Danielle. We took her out on her tricycle one day. We left her alone for a minute while we went into the house to get a warmer coat. There were no brakes on the trike. It rolled down the hill and we never saw her again."

The father laughed each time he told the end of the story. This patient learned to laugh with his father as if it were a joke between them, but secretly he wondered: Could the same thing happen to me? Why didn't Dad go after the tricycle and find his baby? Why was Dad laughing? He felt afraid and learned from this story always "to keep the brakes on" and not to get too far away from the family because they might not come after him.

Some patients report that they are able to discern the initiation of symbiotic behavior: "If you listen carefully, it is possible to hear that Mother sometimes talks in a tone of voice that sounds like a little girl." Some patients refer to this manner of speaking as "baby talk." In addition to the words, with this intonation mothers give out the message that they are in need of being taken care of. Sometimes they will say, in baby talk, that the patients can do something better than they can. The patients feel flattered into helping. The mothers use it only when needed; it is a willful, but not conscious, way of communicating.

Tom came to understand how his mother let him know when he disobeyed a command. He described her as talking to him in a "hurt tone of voice"; she would "prattle about inanities" while totally avoiding the real subject of concern. In either case, it was clear that he had "done wrong," should apologize, and should take better care of his mother. It was impossible to get her to ever consider the real issue. There was no talking about it.

Initially, most patients are completely unaware at a conscious level that these kinds of communications are taking place.

PROMISED REWARDS FOR FOLLOWING THE COMMANDS

The commands appear attractive to patients because they are not just rules; they come with their own set of promised rewards, *if* they can be followed perfectly. The reinforcement can be summarized in the following way. The patients will feel

1. Safe and protected from loss or harm because the parents will always be there.
2. Special.
3. In a close and warm relationship with the parents.
4. That failure produces immediate help.
5. Relieved of the responsibility for the mastery of the difficulties of life beyond taking care of the parents.
6. Rewarded with the promise of special gifts of inheritance.

Even though these rewards appear attractive, both the patients and the parents recognize that something is wrong. Quite simply, if a relationship is valid and meaningful, importuning rewards, punishments, or threats are not needed to maintain it.

SIBLINGS' DIFFERING RESPONSES TO COMMANDS

The children within one family will respond differently to the parental commands, depending upon personality and birth order. Some siblings, frequently the eldest, will try to challenge the symbiosis, fighting back without the aid of psychotherapy. The result may be a serious psychological disturbance, such as a psychotic break in adolescence. Other siblings may overadaptively follow each command to the letter with a superficial "false self," while the "real self" goes into hiding (Winnicott 1965). These siblings are left with the task of reclaiming a real self, but at least they manage to avoid more severe forms of psychotic disturbance. Still other siblings may challenge the system by rebelling passively in a way that is maladaptive to their own growth. For example, they may refuse to attend their chosen Ivy League school because their parents need them to go there. Instead, they attend the local state college because rebelling is "worth it anyway," until they see what is lost in the process. Then in despair, they seek psychotherapy, feeling "caught" as the overadaptive sibling, in trying to expose the parental harm.

When siblings take different routes to handling the enmeshed family ties, it is hard for them to be friends with one another because they have so little in common in their approach to life. Rebellious siblings may scorn their overadaptive siblings for being overly good, whereas overadaptive siblings may disapprove of their more rebellious siblings' defiance.

THE MYTH OF SELF-SUFFICIENCY

Enmeshed families operate by using several myths and distortions that are critical to holding such families together. The *myth of self-sufficiency* is repeatedly presented by patients. It represents the claim that the family can provide any and every relationship; family members are the only ones to understand each other completely (pseudomutuality; see Wynne et al. 1958).

Marianne was told that no one understood her better than her parents, but she nonetheless felt very much misunderstood. She handled this discrepancy by believing that she must indeed be an unusually strange, complex person.

Believing this myth means that patients do not need to have a boyfriend or a girlfriend because the family will provide Saturday evening activities. Likewise, fathers who have a private business do not need an accountant because their sons can be trained to do the necessary paperwork.

The rule is that each member of the family must maintain projects or goals that they cannot complete without the help of other family members. Fathers are especially good at promising to do elaborate projects with their children. A go-cart or doll's house is started with enthusiasm, but the children soon learn that it is likely that these things will never be completed. Outsiders are not supposed to help. In-laws are considered outsiders.

Children are often puzzled by the fact that their parents complain about receiving an invitation to go out and have a good time at a dinner party. The parents act as if they don't want to go; they tell the children that they would rather stay home with the family. Often they do stay home. The children cannot understand why and try to persuade their parents to feel free to leave home and have a good time. Pleasure outside of the home appears to threaten the existence of the myth of self-sufficiency.

Such parents do not feel a need to plan financially for their retirement because they expect their children to remain at home and to repay them by supporting them in their retirement. Even when a family member dies, the other family members fill in for the deceased member. An eldest son replaces his father. If this son considers marriage, his mother may attempt to fill the position of the bride. If a son has a successful psychotherapy experience and separates from the family, the next son in the line will quickly fill his symbiotic place. These families thus act like amoebas, rejecting any particle that feels foreign and engulfing any missing part as if it were not absent. Their family's ability to do this quickly is often deeply hurtful to patients who may have taken an independent step but are not yet prepared for the total rejection they face as a consequence of such action. Attempting to become independent forces patients to face the truly enmeshed nature of their family relationships.

In order to maintain the myth of self-sufficiency, family members are not allowed much latitude for progress. One patient had a recurring dream that lasted for years in which she "watched the waves roll over a stone that never changed." Another patient said, "You walk a tight line all the time because you must succeed and fail only as much as you are directed to, and not fail in helping others within the family." Consequently, everyone in the family must reveal any new relationship so that violations of the myth can be monitored with silent disapproval.

Sometimes external circumstances succeed in taking family members away.

Chad was drafted and sent to England for a six-month tour of duty. He described this period of his life as the most memorable and exciting. He had friends and was able to travel. He was puzzled by the fact that, despite his happiness, he had frequent and unpredictable "crying jags" or "sudden blues" in which he needed to share with his family the things he was doing. He wrote lengthy letters home several times a week as a means of dealing with a strong sense of obligation to stay with the family. He both needed and hated to come home.

THE MYTH OF SELF-RIGHTEOUS PERFECTION

The *myth of self-righteous perfection* involves a false sense of perfection in which parents convey the message that they are omniscient, even deified figures with little knowledge of underlying feelings of insecurity that promulgate the commands. There is never any reason to doubt that what the family does is the right thing. The children learn to strive for perfect obedience. They know when they are "doing wrong," and very little needs to be said directly.

On the surface it looks as if the parents are communicating a standard of excellence with this myth, but it is a standard so impossibly high that it becomes another mechanism for subverting growth. The parents will go out of their way to hide from their children anything that they feel represents trouble so that they can maintain the image of omniscient and omnipotent perfection.

Sometimes these parents flaunt their sense of self-righteousness at the expense of others.

Sally reported that her mother, a seamstress, would come to San Francisco to visit her and buy clothes. Her mother insisted that Sally take her to an expensive store. When they arrived, her mother would criticize the saleswoman's service and the color, quality, or design of the clothes. Sally was forbidden to buy anything for her mother or to pay for her own clothes. Her mother would pay the entire charge. Sally would leave the store wondering how she had managed to pick the wrong store once again and would search harder the next time for a more expensive store. Sally held herself entirely responsible for her mother's unhappiness.

In reality, the parents seemed to be playing out their well-known theme of being perfect, having a lot of money to spend, and viewing the rest of the world as flawed. Actually, the myths of self-sufficiency and self-righteous perfection mandate that Sally in fact allow her seamstress mother to make her clothes.

The myth of self-righteous perfection can be communicated in a variety of different ways. Many patients report being rescued, overindulged, or spoiled by their parents. More normal and responsible interactions with people outside of the family are evaluated negatively. Therefore, the child is encouraged to return home for special or overindulgent treatment. Patients who have learned this distorted view of normal behavior tend to worry excessively about whether or not they are being treated properly; they obsess about what to do if they face mistreatment. Such worry detracts from having a good time. One patient, Arleen, decided to release herself from this constant worry one day by deciding to "be in a good mood for no good reason." She had taken a major step forward by allowing herself this pleasure.

Striving for perfection can be illusory and attractive bait for keeping children at home. The children are led to believe that if they behave perfectly, they will finally achieve the sought-after loving support for growth and acceptance of their own ideas. Unfortunately, loving is used like the carrot before the mule. The children feel that if they just take one more step it might be attained, though in reality it never can be. Invariably the children find that they make just a little mistake, violating one of the family myths or rules. Such children do not really comprehend that no one can ever be perfect, and that their parents never intend to come through with that love because then the children would have what they need to leave home and go on with life. The children have a vague sense of not being able to trust the parents but nonetheless continue to strive for success and to obtain their love and approval. The children's thinking seems very logical: they failed to get the love because they were "not good enough." Other siblings may rebel and give up the game, whereas these children are often the "good" children who try harder than any of the others and believe that they are closer than any of the other siblings to achieving this goal.

Both parents in enmeshed families perpetrate the myth of self-righteous perfection while promising love that they are not capable of giving. Consider the following analogy:

A farmer (parent) with a horse (patient) is in a corral (enmeshed family). The farmer holds out a piece of sugar (love) while walking away from the horse as the horse tries to reach the sugar. They go around and around the corral together, the horse obediently trailing the farmer for the sugar. The horse makes many trips around—surely the next trip will finally yield the sugar? He loses sight of the field outside the corral where the other horses roam freely. He will never get the sugar because if the farmer gave it, the horse would then have the energy and strength to jump the fence.

This analogy helped one patient find and rent an apartment after having lived his adult life with his parents. It is painful for patients to realize that all the trips around the corral have not secured the love but rather have served only to further restrict their growth. It takes perseverance and courage to break through the defense obscuring this knowledge. At times it feels like defeat to the patients to stop plodding around the corral after the sugar.

Tom explained what his relationship with his mother felt like. He said, "We act like two dogs who meet each other on the street and then circle. We never really meet, just look and pass on down the street, both wanting something different, both unable to compromise or fight. I wish that I had had the kind of parents where I felt like I wanted to just be friendly by wagging my tail."

After years of trying and not getting "love," many patients settle instead for managing their financial lives so poorly that they have to borrow money from their parents. The fathers of many impinged-upon adults have managed to be successful in earning a good income. The parents are happy to give money because that perpetuates the dependency. The children are happy to keep the money, without ever paying it back, because it becomes a substitute for love, for support for growth, and for acceptance. At least it is some compensation for efforts toward perfection. The children are unaware that accepting and keeping the money only serves to further entrap them in this dependent and destructive family system. The children are also unaware of the degree to which they have passed up opportunities in order to maintain a state of neediness, to qualify for funds from the parents. It is tragic to see impinged-upon adults refuse to finish a degree or a training program, fail to take a certification examination, or consider turning down a high-paying job because they are so hungry for parental support.

One of the by-products of the myth of self-righteous perfection is patients' disappointment when significant others in their lives are not perfect. Girlfriends or boyfriends are frequently rejected after the first or second date because they are not perfect. Therapists make a mistake, such as being late or offering a poorly timed interpretation, explanation, or clarification, and the patients wonder if the psychotherapy will be doomed to failure. The myth of self-righteous perfection not only holds the family together but makes it extremely difficult to find outside relationships that meet the supposed criteria of perfection. One patient, Ron, seemed relieved to hear me say, "Even if you did meet a girlfriend who was perfect, she probably wouldn't be a good match anyway, because it is impossible for *you* to be perfect!"

During the psychotherapy, I sometimes encourage patients to "be bad" and arrive late because a phone conversation or a job interview was more important for their growth than being on time for a psychotherapy hour. Patients are further surprised that I do not expect the psychotherapy hour to be perfect. Even with diligent work, mistakes will be made; they can be discussed and corrected, and the work will be sufficient to accomplish the task. Patients often experience relief in understanding this new concept. It reduces the constant pressure they feel to be exactly on time, watch their behavior, choose their words carefully. They can begin to relax and spontaneously say what they really feel.

When the myth of self-righteous perfection is realized as an impossible condition, a sense of self-acceptance previously unknown to the patients enters the psychotherapy relationship. However, this myth is very difficult to leave behind; it has been deeply ingrained. One patient said to me, "If it is really true, as you say, that I don't have to be perfect, it is as if you are presenting me with a fairy tale. I never imagined it could be real."

The myth of self-righteous perfection can cause trouble in a different way. Because of the parental power they have experienced, patients enter the world trusting too much and with little experience in detecting and handling trouble. If a situation in the real world feels bad to them, they tend to assume instead that others are perfect and that they are wrong. They are not easily able to perceive exploitation from others and may need to be taught that some streets are not safe for walking. They are vulnerable to working too hard for others and feel unable to correct the situation with assertion or a confrontation until it is too late.

The emergence of the myth of self-righteous perfection in the therapeutic relationship enables patients to deal with it. It is hard for patients to realize that they no longer need to strive for this false sense of perfection.

Tanya shared with me a moment in which the good and bad parts of herself became integrated into a single whole person. She was no longer a slave to the myth of self-righteous perfection. She was sharing a letter that she had received from a friend. Their relationship had been strained for a long time because of some mistakes each of them had made. They had just begun to make contact with each other again. She said, "I always believed that if I did anything wrong with my parents, that they would do something terrible to me. I have done something that was very difficult for this person to handle. Yet, she still seems to accept both the good and bad parts of me. She seems to want to continue the relationship. I feel moved."

It is harder still to realize the parents' imperfections. At first, patients hope that the therapist can make all their parents' imperfections disappear. Then they could justify continuing a closely enmeshed relationship with family and avoid the difficulties of real life.

MISINFORMATION

In addition to the commands and the myths, some parents of impinged-upon adults find it necessary to provide misinformation to their children to keep them from leaving home. It becomes the therapist's job to replace this misinformation with liberating and accurate facts. It is difficult to ascertain the extent to which the parents believe this information themselves, or whether they are conscious of misleading their children. It often serves to put fear into their children, making them afraid to take the next growth step. Following are some examples:

Dan's mother tells him that he can make a woman pregnant by lying on a beach next to her in a bathing suit. He then becomes afraid to ask a girl for a slow dance because he fears that the bodily contact will make her pregnant.

Judy's mother tells her that something bad will happen to her by the end of the day if she doesn't stop giggling. She makes sure not to laugh on any day that has a special event scheduled for her because she is afraid she will not get to attend.

Alice becomes afraid to go horseback riding because her mother says that the posting on the horse causes her menstrual cramps.

THE TYRANNY OF TIME AND TIME AS INFINITE

Regularly scheduled appointments starting on time allow patients to experience their past feelings regarding their parents' use of time. Many patients report that their parents handled being on time in rigid ways. Their mother or father usually had a strong, unshakable need to arrive either early or late.

Mary's father collected the entire family and insisted that they arrive anywhere from twenty to thirty minutes early. The family was then expected to stay in the car and listen to a ball game with him. It never occurred to Mary to ask if she could get out and go for a walk.

Alice's father insisted on being twenty to thirty minutes late. That meant that the family assembled together in the living room to wait for him. No one could do anything else during that time.

As the feelings of anger about this abuse of time surface, patients often need to come to the hour either late or early to assert their own sense of independence.

Some parents also communicate a second misconception regarding time. They lead patients to believe that time is infinite and that there is no hurry about applying to college, dating, marrying, or having a family. One patient was very surprised to hear me say, "Perhaps you need to give this matter more attention, because your clock may be running out." The patient responded, "But Mother told me I could marry all the way up to the age of 60." Patients often have aspirations for a certain career—for example, getting into medical school—but no sense that there is any time restriction on attaining it.

THE MYTH OF AN ETERNAL, TROUBLE-FREE WORLD
   VERSUS REALITY

The myths of self-sufficiency and self-righteous perfection, and the tyranny of time, combine to make the *myth of an eternal, trouble-free world*. Some patients have a mistaken sense, although they know better, that they will never die as long as their parents are alive and they (the patients) stay close to home. They are shaken out of this notion only when a parent becomes seriously ill. These patients have not learned to consider the finiteness of life. The reflections of one patient fairly define this myth of an eternal, trouble-free world:

I always thought that I would be safe as long as my mother was alive and I was with her. I believed I never needed to worry about anything. I never considered my death or hers. Now my mother is ill. For the first time, I realize that she could die. What will happen to my safe world? Can I survive without her? Then you [the therapist] told me that there was no such thing as a safe world. All of a sudden this week, I have been noticing things that actually could happen. I may never see the person I spoke to yesterday again; my children and I could be involved in a car accident; there could be a bad fire. I feel depressed; I don't like reality. Do other people not like it? It is too late for me to turn back to the way I was before, but I liked it better the old way. Is there nothing I can do about this uncertainty?

This patient was dealing with childhood feelings and the defense of splitting. She had previously seen the world as "all good," and now she saw it as "all bad" (Grotstein 1981, Masterson 1976, Rinsley 1982). She had yet to integrate these two views into one reasonable truth.

She could see no benefit in recognizing uncertainty and finiteness as parts of life. I suggested that this new awareness helped her to take good care of herself and her family; to minimize the chance of accident; to maximize the quality of her interactions with others so that her relationships would feel as complete as possible; to take care of problems promptly when they arose; and to formulate a realistic plan for her life based upon her full awareness that the time of her ultimate death is unknown. The tragedy of this myth is that it had eliminated her awareness of the need to take these actions.

THE MYTH OF COMPLIMENTS

The *myth of compliments* refers to the fact that parents of impinged-upon adults give what seem like compliments but are not. These "compliments" are, instead, orders or directives about how to behave within the enmeshed family. This fact becomes clear when patients recoil from any of the therapist's comments that might be construed as complimentary and become wary of the relationship with the therapist.

These patients take any expression of support as an order. If they feel unable to comply with such an order, they feel inadequate, anxious, and afraid of rejection. Therefore, over the years the patients learn to avoid any orders by turning down all compliments. Unfortunately, the patients lose valuable support from outsiders that should rightfully have gone into building a solid self-concept.

A situation that warrants a compliment for a job well done often receives parental undermining instead. Therefore, patients learn to be wary of and to avoid situations warranting a compliment. One patient experienced this kind of undermining when he was five years old:

Alan's father had been away on a trip and was returning home in the evening with one of his colleagues. The colleague received a phone call. Alan, at age five, answered the phone and memorized the information correctly. When his father came home, Alan proudly ran out to the car to deliver the message, even though it was raining. His father listened and then cut in with "Where are your boots and your raincoat? See how things fall apart here when Daddy is away!" Alan knew that he did not own boots or a raincoat! His father reacted to Alan's mastery with feelings of inadequacy that forced his father to assert his supremacy by scolding. Alan wisely avoided such situations in the future.

A real compliment occurs obliquely in only two ways. The parents will express pride in their children's behavior or in how the children look only to outsiders when the children are not within earshot. If a compliment is given directly to children about their looks, it tends to be said in an oblique way. For example, a patient who was wearing a new dress was told, "That dress looks nice" rather than, "You look pretty in that new dress." The compliment goes to the dress. The children never get the compliment directly because the parents sense and fear that their remarks will promote confidence and independence.

Compliments from therapists that support growth may activate the patients' internalized parental attack. For example, I commented to a patient that he seemed to be a man who knew how to be gentle, especially when he related to women sexually. His intrapsychic parental voice made the compliment negative by telling him, "That means you are probably a homosexual." When I expressed to another patient, Mary, that she seemed to be able to trust me, she confessed that a voice inside her warned, "Look out! You are being gullible." At first, patients will tend to hear these comments from within and not say anything about them.

PARENTAL PUNISHMENT AND THREATENED ABANDONMENT

Punishment is frequently the vehicle by which parental sabotage is delivered. It is as if, instead of letting a baby bird fly away from the nest when it is ready, the mother bird finds a way to clip its wings. Patients feel punished for something they have done.

Jim was a talented sculptor. During his psychotherapy he brought me some miniature sculptures that he felt "compelled" to create over and over again. He did not like them; they made him feel "uncomfortable," but he "had to do them." The sculptures were a series of people wearing something like life jackets that he called "life supports." The life jackets were in the process of being pulled away. The people looked like they were gasping for life and were falling down. He said that was exactly the way he felt. Every time he took a step forward, he risked the punishment of having "the life supports pulled away from his body."

Martha took a new job and started talking about moving out of her parents' home, into her own condominium apartment. One day when she came home from work, she discovered her parents obviously waiting for her. Her mother had experienced some difficulty with asthma and had spent a portion of the day at the hospital. As Martha walked into the room, her father angrily held up the hospital identification bracelet that had been placed on her mother's arm and said, "Look what happened to your mother while you were gone!" His tone of voice implied that if she had not been gone the extra hours at her new job, this would not have happened. Martha felt so guilty because of this accusation that she canceled her appointment with me in order to take her mother to the doctor again. She left a message that said, "Family medical emergency." By this time, her mother was not in need of further medical attention, but Martha feared she might be the cause of both her mother's death and her own death (because she was symbiotically dependent upon her mother).

When children are young, parents tend to punish by threatening abandonment. Sometimes this can be carried to a point that is extremely frightening for children. The children then try to avoid such abuse with overcompliant behavior.

Sarah, age six, was not acting according to her parents' wishes. Her parents asked if she liked living at home. She responded honestly, no. They then asked if she wished to leave home. She answered yes. Her parents dressed her and gave her a lunch box containing a few pieces of food. Then they drove her to the bus station and let her out. They waited, hidden in the parking lot. She decided that there was nothing to do but to get on the next bus. She did. Her parents followed and rescued her just before the bus departed. This is a more literal abandonment than many parents dare try with their children (Masterson 1976, Rinsley 1982).

Parental abandonment can also be expressed to adult patients.

Mary got a new and prestigious job. She went out to lunch with her parents to celebrate and tell them about it. Her father responded by saying that he planned to change his trust accounts. He would leave all of his assets to the other three siblings because she would not need the money anymore, now that she had such a good job. Mary became upset, having learned to accept money as the only substitute for family intimacy.

Parental subversion of a growth step may take the form of constant irrelevant criticism, which is then internalized. Therefore, when patients complete an independent growth step, they anticipate a negative attack for doing something wrong. One patient anticipated the pleasure of picking up the bound copies of her doctoral dissertation. However, instead of feeling happy, she felt sad, depressed, and uneasy about what she had done wrong.

Patients have made real progress when they understand that parental sabotage means that the parents recognize that their child has taken a step forward. Sabotage takes on a new meaning as a backward compliment indicating that the child's forward progress is being noticed by the parents. One patient, Martha, spoke clearly to this issue.

"Whenever I wanted something, my parents said, 'You can do without it.' That's one of the key ways they kept me from growing. I now understand that my mother said that because she didn't want me to leave her, and my father said it because he was afraid that I would succeed better than he. But as a kid, the only thing I felt was that I didn't deserve it. Their attack really worked. I felt cut back. Now I understand why I always felt sick to my stomach when I saw a Japanese bonsai tree. I can't stand to see growth stunted."

Sabotage sometimes comes disguised as help, which makes it exceptionally confusing.

A father, well known for his undermining behavior, helped his son fix the son's dirt bike. Unconsciously, the father tightened one of the parts down so tight that the son couldn't get the bike to run.

Matthew decided to move away from his family on the west coast, to the east coast. The night before he left, he had "the most frightening dream of my whole life." During a portion of the dream, he was being chased by an ambulance with a blind driver. He could not get away. The ambulance was a symbol of the pathologic "rescue from life" his parents insisted on giving him. The blind driver symbolized the reckless pursuit by parents who could not even see who he was, or what they were doing. He was able to escape, an ending which gave him the courage to leave home.

Some patients are born with exceptional talent, making it difficult to fail. They must employ their talents to find ways to subvert their own creativity so that they can continue to live within their families.

Jason was a professional horn player. He created for himself a fear that incorporated Mephistopheles. He imagined that if he played the next note correctly, played a perfect performance, or went away from home to give a concert, he would become possessed by the devil. It was a way of locating the destructive parts of his relationship with his parents outside the family. This fear became so intense that, for a time, he had to have a member of the family stay with him at all times. He was not aware of his self-defeating behavior. His family stayed home with him rather than insist that he seek psychological help. Even when hypnotic treatment had helped him to overcome the fear of Mephistopheles, he remained fearful that this obsession would return. It was not until he understood his relationship to his family that the fear no longer dominated him.

All forms of abandonment feel real to children. Some of the parents' threats of illness and suicide even seem believable to the therapist. It has become clear, however, through the years with this kind of patient that the abandonment claims are, with rare exceptions, mere threats. The parent does indeed survive after the patient achieves a separation from the family. The threat is not likely to be carried out because parents need their offspring too much to actually abandon them. Patients can do anything reasonable with their lives, and their parents will still be there. In fact, the sabotage generally ceases as soon as the parents realize that the patient is no longer influenced by it. The patients achieve their goals and the parents begin, instead, to get their psychological needs met by feeling like successful parents.

Most impinged-upon adults are understandably hungry for appreciation from others. They want someone to celebrate a success, someone able to say thank you when a job is well done. They seem insatiable in this regard. They must learn that people in their present lives may not be aware of their past deprivation.

If the parental undermining is extremely severe, patients may decide to use extreme measures to avoid their rage about the demands of enmeshed family ties. Patients have tried (1) homosexuality as a means of keeping away from women like their mother; (2) suicide attempts as a way of saying, "None of this matters. I am already dead." (3) creating a vivid utopian afterlife; (4) collecting large stuffed animals, symbolizing warm cuddly creatures to be close to without fear; and (5) making a vow never to be employed in a job requiring work with people, for example, to work only with computers.

THE FEAR OF ENGULFMENT

The fear of abandonment and rejection is the most common one among impinged-upon adults. This fear manifests itself as anxiety attacks in which patients fear that they will be abandoned by the therapist and by their friends. A less common fear is that of engulfment. This fear results from a disturbed relationship between mothers and infants. Patients react to this kind of violation of boundaries in a completely different way. Patients fear that when they decide to take a step forward with their life, it is really not their step. They feel that the therapist made them do it. Patients feel subtly brainwashed or swallowed up by the therapist rather than fear of abandonment (Grotstein 1981). One patient, Alan, had a vivid experience that illustrates this fear.

"I was lying in bed, on the edge of sleep. I felt something fluid creeping up behind me. It felt like a nameless form. It was going to envelope me. I realized the form was my mother. I felt intense fear but made the conscious decision for the first time in my life to lie still and see what happened.

"I fell asleep. My fear of being consumed did not occur. I realized, through this experience, that I had felt a need to keep moving to avoid being enveloped. Previously, I felt unable to move slowly and deliberately with life. Instead, I acted impulsively and impatiently, often making decisions that I regretted in the long term. I had felt a need to keep moving to avoid the nameless form."

Alan explained the difference between the fear of abandonment and engulfment by saying, "My fear is not being told to leave, but turning my back. I feel utter loneliness when I feel engulfed. I don't exist by myself. I can't get away or out to anyone else."

Alan wanted "attention in the form of support and guidance." He experienced his mother's engulfing as dangerous as a "duck who headed her brood toward an alligator."

Dan decided to cope with his fear of engulfment by doing nothing with his life. He concluded, "If I have nothing to tell my parents when they call, then they might be forced to leave me alone. I am willing to give up living to keep them off my back." He had never been given permission to set limits for his parents' behavior. He described their form of engulfment as follows: "I found a small gift for my parents. I knew that it was something that they would like and I really wanted them to have it. But I was afraid to send it to them because I knew the gift would immediately activate a phone call from them. They would jump back into my life."

After much working through of these issues, he decided to act for himself and bought a piece of property. He was afraid to tell his parents because, he said, "they will want to jump in and design the house for me and I will lose the property as my own." He was afraid not to tell them because, when they eventually found out, he knew that they would feel "panicky" about the fact that they had been excluded. Then they would, he said, "bug me even more."

Dan had a dream in which he was planting a new garden. Every time he made a hole for a new plant, an oversized bullfrog jumped out. They sat around him until there were so many that a friend said, "Look out or you will step on one and hurt it." He recognized that the planting of the garden represented his new life, and that the frogs were his parents "jumping all over" him. His understanding helped him design more effective ways to communicate with them. For instance, he decided to buy an answering machine for his telephone and to send a postcard periodically. This way, his parents could feel included, but he had gained control over his contact with them and what he said.

THE VIOLATION OF BOUNDARIES

Enmeshed family relationships involve constant violation of psychological boundaries.

Rachael said that she would prefer to cease any further mention about her parents in her psychotherapy because she felt so compelled to tell her mother everything that was said. It did not occur to her that she could continue her dialogue with me and not inform her mother.

Daniel came into his mother's kitchen. His mother commented, "I feel warm." She then walked over to Daniel and began to untuck his shirt, assuming that her son felt the same way.

Ann's parents traveled across the country to visit her for the second time in a three-year period. They came to the door, opened it, and walked in without knocking.

Letters written home by patients are frequently passed on indiscriminately to extended family members. There is no sense that a letter might be private or meant for only one person; the family has only one elastic boundary.

There seems to be a relationship between obesity and the violation of psychological boundaries. Some patients report that they feel anywhere from fifteen to thirty pounds overweight. Try as they might, they have a difficult time losing the extra pounds. Some are still living at home with parents who stock the refrigerator with lots of irresistible high-caloric foods. Several feelings are commonly expressed by these patients:

"If I am fatter, I feel like I have more of a boundary between me and my parents."

"No matter how much I weigh, I feel like a piece of glass. My parents can always see inside."

"Fat is ugly and keeps me from leaving home."

"Food is a tempting substitute for the loving that is missing."

Once they become aware of these misconceptions and understand that the violation of boundaries is psychological rather than physical, they are often able to embark on a weight-loss program with tangible success.

In what other ways can young children handle the violation of boundaries? Guilty adults tell a lot of stories about the "bad" things they did in childhood. Some of them found something outrageous to do in secret, mainly to prove to themselves that they were something more than an overcompliant extension of their parents. Some children get tremendous pleasure out of hiding from their parents the fact that they steal. If their parents do find out, the children refuse to admit the crime. It is not so much that they fear parental punishment; instead, they want to prove their separateness.

When patients are able to understand their actions in this light, they can view their childhood experiences with a new respect for themselves. Most impinged-upon adults have been good children who are excessively embarrassed about the few transgressions they have committed.

PATIENTS' RELATIONSHIPS WITH SIBLINGS

Impinged-upon adults appear to have a higher than normal incidence of siblings with severe psychological difficulty, often manifesting in a psychotic break during adolescence. These disturbed siblings are often the children who fight back hardest against enmeshed family ties because they accurately perceive the ways in which they are damaging to growth. Patients find these siblings intimidating but watch and learn that in fighting back, more is lost than is gained. Such siblings may commit suicide, may never leave home, may maintain a marginal existence outside of the home, may live in a state hospital, or their whereabouts may be unknown to the family. It remains unclear to what extent this major disturbance is organic and happens incidental to the environmental problems of enmeshed family ties, is environmentally induced by inadequate parenting, or requires a combination of both factors. This higher ratio of severely disturbed siblings suggests that environment may be a sizable contributing factor.

As patients achieve separateness and mastery over their own lives, it is usually necessary to spend considerable time in the therapy sorting out their feelings about a disturbed sibling. The patients may be afraid to succeed because it will hurt the sibling who is doing poorly with life. The patients feel as if this sibling suffered more than they did and feel obligated not to add to that suffering. They feel this sibling's pain and loss and feel tempted to stay behind and help. It is difficult for these patients to accept the fact that their need to fail will not help their disturbed sibling to function better. Their concern is well founded because the parents have urged the remaining siblings, in subtle ways, not to succeed because it will expose and embarrass the disturbed sibling or make him or her feel left out.

Sometimes the disturbed sibling is creative, talented, and much younger than the patient. If the patient succeeds in leaving home, he or she often has to work through the guilt and grief resulting from the inability to take this younger sibling along. The patient wants to exercise unrealistic, almost superhuman powers to release this younger child.

Patients have one additonal problem in relation to their more disturbed sibling: they have an exceptionally strong fear of expressing emotion because they are afraid that feelings will erupt out of control as they did during the sibling's psychotic break and will again make that sibling "crazy." Therefore, these patients tend to be more guarded in the expression of affect and are in need of more psychological education, encouragement, and support, to enable them to use emotion in a constructive and manageable way. Patients with a disturbed sibling harbor a fear that their offspring will inherit their sibling's problems.

Siblings who are not severely disturbed band together to be supportive of one another. Siblings can validate and help one another to realize that their feelings are legitimate. They may stand in for one another, taking turns being the focus of the problem communications from the parents. They act much as a flight of birds traveling in formation: when the leader gets tired, he or she drops back and another member takes over.

Sometimes one sibling is much older and takes on the job of parenting younger siblings. The younger children may not be aware of this privileged parenting until the older sibling goes away from home. The younger children do not understand the depth of their loss until they realize years later in psychotherapy that an older sibling provided the best parenting they received.

When patients separate from their family, they may run into difficulty maintaining a relationship with siblings who remain enmeshed with the parents. The siblings who stay with the parents may view the patients as defectors from the family, and the parents may encourage separateness between them. These patients may have to settle for a distant and superficial friendship because there is so little common ground.

CONCLUSION

Enmeshed parents must forego mature interaction with their adult children because they are unable to relinquish the position of power and control that maintains the entanglement. If the parents visit their children, they prefer to buy their own food or go to a restaurant and pay for everyone's meals, instead of eating the food pepared specifically for them by their children. They have an extremely difficult time shopping when their grown children are buying something for them. If the children succeed in paying for the gift, it may well be left unused for some time. These parents prefer to continue to buy gifts for their children.

At an unconscious level patients already have much of the basic information contained in this book. As patients come to understand their difficulty, they can look back on their past creative projects and see glimpses of feelings about past relationships (Mahler 1975). Difficulty with separation emerges as a consistent theme in these patients' stories, poetry, sculpture, and drawings, even at an early age. Sometimes these projects of the past find their way into the therapist's office. The patients' creativity has usually been redirected to defend against or articulate an attempt to resolve the unresolved issues of development, separation, and intimacy.

Melinda gave an address at her high school commencement. The theme of her speech concerned a bird trying to get out of its egg. Someone came along and helped the young bird by cracking the shell; but the shell cracker had inadvertently robbed the bird of the strength it would have acquired fighting its own way out of the egg. The bird was unable to fly properly. Melinda advised her audience not to rescue each other to such an extent that opportunities to conquer the hurdles of living are taken away.

CHAPTER 5

Separation Issues and Process

During the course of psychotherapy, patients change their view of their parents. First, patients lift the denial surrounding the pathological interactions sustaining enmeshment. Then patients see, for the first time, the limitations that result from the maintenance of a close family. Patients then recognize the commands and myths, feel anger, see why their parents imposed such restrictions on the family, and gradually turn to the task of repairing the incompleteness within themselves. This chapter explores the step-by-step change in thinking and feeling necessary for the birth of a self.

THE DIFFERENCE BETWEEN BEING NEEDED AND BEING LOVED

The biggest and most painful issue that must be clarified with patients is the difference between being *needed* (psychologically) and being *loved*. Impinged-upon adults rarely use love to describe the relationship between themselves and their parents. For example, they say, "My parents *needed* me" or "We were *very close*." These are the words that describe the symbiotic dependency of children who were never allowed to grow up.

One hallmark of this phenomenon is that the parents are frequently referred to as "Mummy" and "Daddy" rather than by a more mature appellation. Retention of these childhood titles by adult patients suggests that they still feel like children in the family of origin rather than like adults at the head of their own family. Likewise, parents reinforce dependency by speaking of their toddlers as infants and of their grown offspring as children rather than as sons or daughters.

Patients describe their relationship with their parents in several ways.

Alice, an articulate female lawyer, observed, "To feel weak, inadequate, and special at the same time is meant to send you to the loony bin."

Tom reflected, "My mother gave the gift of life, but only on the condition that I serve her needs before my own. I have spent my life at her altar."

Alice said sarcastically, as she showed me a copy of the family Christmas photograph, "See, I am one of my parents' Christmas tree ornaments."

Another patient, Karen, said, "My parents' bottom line was always 'What is yours is ours, what is mine is mine.' "

Jan's mother came to visit. The visit went well at first, and her mother was even able to be supportive of the new home Jan had bought. Then some out-of-town friends called asking if they could stop by briefly for a visit. Her mother's mood suddenly changed; she became cold and distant. When the friends arrived they began to chat with Jan and her mother. Her mother disappeared into the bedroom. Jan went after her and asked, "I don't understand; What is wrong?" Her mother responded, "You don't care about me anymore. I should have gone back home. I can see that I am not needed. You shouldn't have invited them to visit when I was already here."

This mother's comments reveal her need for her symbiotic rather than loving relationship with her daughter, and her extreme discomfort in watching her daughter relate to anyone else.

Some parents are able to say "I love you" as part of their

superficial knowledge of the permissions. Other parents apparently do not use these words.

Philosophers, psychologists, authors, and poets have all attempted to define love, yet its meaning remains elusive. It is necessary to conclude, however, that loving is a more mature phenomenon than the interaction that takes place within patients' families. That is not to say that these patients receive less than the best that their parents have to offer in terms of shelter, clothes, education, or money. Their parents often excel in meeting such basic needs. However, a prerequisite for loving is a sense of wholeness and separateness as a person, with enough respect and responsibility for oneself to feel comfortable being intimate with someone else. Loving includes being able to respect and support another person's growth. Loving implies reciprocal healthy giving without demanding or obligating the recipient to respond out of guilt. Sullivan sees intimacy occurring "when a person feels that the welfare of another individual is as important as his own well-being" (Chapman 1978, p. 204).

The interactions reported in therapy hours suggest that the patients were deprived of mature loving. This is painful to realize, but the hurt is mitigated by the patients' new understanding that love was not withheld because they were unlovable but because their parents did not feel psychologically complete enough to engage in mature intimacy, either with their children or with each other.

In addition, impinged-upon adults have difficulty with caring about themselves because they do not feel any more psychologically complete than did their unentitled parents. Impinged-upon adults have remained an extension of their parents. If they are able to face their incompleteness and self-sabotaging behavior, they find that they can create a whole, separate self that enables them to respect and love both themselves and other people. This is a formidable task. It is one of the reasons why psychotherapy takes a long time.

Patients describe incidents that suggest that they are aware of this lack of loving.

Richard did a fine job with a number of difficult interviews and secured a top-notch job with a good salary. He was competing against many qualified applicants. When he went home, he was surprised that he felt no joy but instead wept for hours. He realized he would no longer need his parents' money, which he had been accepting for years as a substitute for love. He wept because he felt that no one had ever loved him and that the new job meant that no one ever would. He was grieving the loss of his only substitute for love.

The issue of loving and needing is further complicated when separation issues get mixed up with oedipal issues. Sometimes mothers of an impinged-upon adult, instead of providing love and support, teach their sons to be totally dependent upon the mothers' adoration as a substitute for a positive sense of self they should have helped their sons build. This adoration is never fully given but is held out like a carrot, subtly and secretly promised in the form of an eventual, perfect sexual union. The sons continue to return for this forbidden fruit as their way of reaching for an external adoration they can never seem to obtain within themselves. When the mothers continue to tease but never offer their sexuality, the sons are constantly frustrated and may turn to various forms of perverse sexual experiences as a substitute, acting out both their longing and their anger at this frustrating situation. No other woman looks as perfect sexually as their mother. In addition, the sons cannot like themselves well enough to become intimate with anyone else. Unless a psychotherapist intervenes, the mothers continue to promulgate their perfect image. Their sons return to them for life and never marry. It is extremely difficult for sons to admit that this interaction is taking place and give up their angry quest for their mothers.

MANIFESTATIONS OF PATIENTS' ANGER

Impinged-upon adults become angry about the commands, the lack of loving, and their sense of failure. This anger originates long before the psychotherapy, though it may be blocked from conscious awareness. In fact, impinged-upon adults are often puzzled by seemingly unrelated external circumstances that activate their anger. For instance, they feel more infuriated by rush-hour traffic than the situation warrants. The slowed mass of cars feels like their parents stopping them from going on with life. They have the same reaction to extended waiting for a doctor's visit. They usually laugh when the similarity is pointed out to them.

What can impinged-upon adults do with their anger before they understand it? Prior to psychotherapy, they tend to choose pathological alternatives that compromise their lives in some way. Each action serves the purpose of trying to escape the commands, act out the anger, or express it through rebellion. Some impinged-upon adults blow up over trivial things. Others staunchly and routinely rebel by refusing to do something small that would help life to run more smoothly.

Some impinged-upon-adult patients are fortunate in their ability to rediscover the anger that they have been forbidden to express. It comes out in the psychotherapy hour, in dreams, in behavior toward friends and co-workers, or sometimes trans-ferentially. It is not as frightening as the patients might have expected. It is the therapist's responsibility to see to it that anger is brought into awareness in small, manageable amounts.

Other impinged-upon-adult patients have learned to ex-press their anger in an unconscious, passive manner or by acting out in a way that results in maintaining failure. This anger is harder to reach. The therapist often senses the passive expres-sion of anger in the therapy hour. The therapist may observe patients understanding the content and process of each session but not doing anything more with their life than before. These patients prefer to let things ride with no obvious sense of discom-fort. The therapist begins to feel frustrated, as if the patients were pulling against the therapist. The patients plead innocent and ask the therapist to say it again, even though the patients can articulate easily what has transpired in the therapy. In fact, patients may mildly enjoy the confusion and not want to under-stand why they are not using the new knowledge. The therapist feels pulled to work harder. Nothing happens.

Gradually, the confusion subsides, and the therapist learns from each patient's acting out. Patients have themselves pro-vided the following reasons why they have acted out their anger by failing in life. Some patients fail

1. because they prefer the defense of remaining stagnant rather than experiencing the anger they feel about being held back.

2. so that "nothing is going on" for their parents to sabotage.
3. because they are afraid to succeed, for fear that their past deprivations will be forgotten by their parents.
4. to prove that their parents failed.
5. because they do not want their parents to "live off" their success. They wish to pay back their parents by their failure in a deeply retaliative gesture, even if it means sacrificing part of their own life experience. They are not aware of the fact that this sort of retaliation ties them down as severely as overcompliance.
6. because they desire the attention and contact they feel they have learned to get through failure.
7. because they fear that success will take them away from the supportive therapeutic relationship. (Most patients realize the supportive component in a therapist's confrontation. They fear that success would take away the need for this kind of support.)

Any one of the above ways of handling anger makes the psychotherapy extremely confusing and difficult for the therapist to manage. Furthermore, if therapists collude with patients in this avoidance, the trouble is compounded, since the patients have already heavily invested in keeping their anger disguised.

Amy knew that she was resisting her anger but did not yet understand why. In the middle of feelings of despair and sadness she said, "I am pitiful in my inability to do anything with my life. My resistance is like a piece of armor surrounding me. I cannot find the door or a crack of light to see my anger. Everything looks dark, hidden by the resistance."

Later, Amy succeeded in working through her anger and went on to explain herself to me. A summary of her thoughts from two psychotherapy hours follows:

I am spiteful. By that I mean I am willing to hurt myself to get back at someone else. I am angry because I have never been in control of my life. Other people have used it for their own benefit. I was taught as a child that a good person is someone who does things only for other people. A bad person considers her own needs and that is selfish.

I'm thinking of an example. As a seven-year-old girl, I heard the ice cream truck come down the street for the first time in our neighborhood. I got my money and ran outside and got myself a cone. I felt so proud that I could do that all by myself. When I went back into the house, my parents came down on me really hard because I had forgotten to ask anyone else in the family if they wanted a cone too, as if they couldn't hear the ice cream truck themselves. I remember feeling so confused and deflated.

I'm so mad and spiteful that I will even hurt myself to get even. The phrase 'taking charge of your own life' has only been a useless jingle to me. I've had to spend my life resisting what other people need me to do for them. I never got a chance to evaluate my life beyond that simple principle. It never occurred to me that I *could* do something I wanted or something that someone else wanted me to do, if it also happened to be good for me.

Several hours later, she went on to define her passive-aggressive anger further as "deliberate incompetence." She came into her hour both angry and crying. She had just been taught to use a complex typewriter at work, and she had done extremely well. She was proud of herself but also realized that if her father had been the one to teach her, she would be doing very badly. Through her tears, she blurted out, while she stamped her foot on the floor for emphasis,

My father kept trying to make me learn to play chess. He wanted me to play so that he could beat me. He would have taught me badly so I never would have had the knowledge I needed to win. He also needed me to play because it was an educated thing for me to do and he would be embarrassed if I couldn't. But I beat him. I refused to play!

If I was angry, I was made to feel helpless and incompetent. No one ever asked why. By developing my deliberate incompetence, I got to be angry passively. I got to make him feel helpless and incompetent. I also got to protect my talent from his humiliation. If I had done well with the game, I would have been sent away as if I were a leper.

If patients succeed in working through their anger, there is often a period of time when they have to endure feeling angry, all of the time, at everything. During this period, it is important for therapists to urge patients to take especially good care of themselves. Sometimes the anger turns inward, and patients feel hopeless about continuing life or the enormous task of psychotherapy. There is usually no definite suicide plan but a temporary feeling of wanting to get away from the pain. It becomes easy for patients to run a red light, for example. The support and the therapist's availability by phone during this period are helpful and sometimes essential.

A difficult circumstance can occur when patients act out their anger, accumulated from many parental interactions, transferentially with the therapist. This acting out serves patients as a defense so that they can avoid conscious awareness of their anger.

Jim, a teenager, was angry at his mother for failing to give him the love and support to which he felt entitled. He tried unsuccessfully to engage her interest in him by lounging around the house, doing nothing, hoping that she would notice him and urge him to go out and play hockey. Then he tried for sexual love, instead, by being flirtatious. When he discovered that his therapist was also unwilling to provide either kind of love, he acted out by punishing-type behavior. For a time, he tried to "destroy the psychotherapy" by preventing a successful outcome. He claimed, "The psychotherapy work you do with me is the only thing of yours that I can reach out to hurt." He allowed the psychotherapy to stay in a state of impasse for a number of sessions, while we wrestled with understanding the reason for this behavior. Understanding allowed him to give up the punishment.

Tom felt the need to rebel in therapy in the same way that he had with his mother. He would guess what he thought I wanted him to do. Then he would state the guess as his own feelings. When I reflected the feeling back to him, he took it as a command from me and rebelled against it. In the process, he became very confused about what he wanted to do for himself. He was doing things he didn't wish to do in order to continue to rebel. It did not seem to matter that his life was not moving in the direction he wanted it to.

These bouts of anger can be long-standing and tiresome for the therapist to handle; understanding makes the critical difference. In the process, the therapist has to suspend the wish for progress. If patients detect that the therapist needs them to get well, their rebellion tends to be stronger and lasts longer.

PATIENTS' CONCERN ABOUT THEIR PARENTS

Patients are concerned not only about themselves and their ability to survive as separate people, but they also worry excessively about their parents. Patients are afraid that their parents will die (psychologically), as maternal command 11 predicts, if they disobey a command.

During the separation–individuation process, patients frequently report a period of time when their parents respond with a recurring illness of unusual severity. The parents will dwell both on this problem and on their aging, as a means of re-engaging the patients in the old ways. Sometimes the parents threaten that they might die while the patients are away (Masterson and Rinsley 1975). The patients feel worried and guilty but continue to progress, and the parents eventually feel well again.

Nancy received a call from her mother, who sounded cheerful and well at the beginning of the telephone conversation. Then her mother requested that Nancy come and spend the night. Nancy responded, "I don't know yet, I'll have to see how I feel." Each time she gave this kind of response, her mother sounded "sicker," complaining of a bad headache and the large number of pills she was having to take.

In reality, most parents benefit from patients' emerging independence. The parents' exhausting crises, which occurred with regularity and forced the patients to remain psychologically attached, often decrease in frequency. Ill parents may learn to seek more appropriate medical treatment for their illnesses, so that episodes of sickness are less frequent and severe. Toward the end of psychotherapy, patients may be approached by friends of the family who comment that their parents are looking very well, in fact much better than usual. When patients hear this, they know that their parents are beginning to benefit from the separate lives that the patients have achieved.

In addition, parents have frequently denied themselves objects of pleasure, such as a new car or a summer home. The money has been spent instead to pay the children to stay enmeshed. The parents may have also denied themselves fun items because these luxuries were in conflict with the image of needing help that they wished to present to their children. It is gratifying to see patients' growth allow them to turn down the "payoff" for security and instead encourage their parents to buy that new car or take that trip to Hawaii. When the parents can accept this invitation, they also make possible a new relationship with their offspring in which their grown children can meaningfully encourage and advise them. The patients once again help their parents, but this time, in a constructive, positive way for them both.

Donald, a competent banker, took over the husband role in his family of origin when his father died in a plane accident. Then he began to date and came into psychotherapy to work through the issues preventing his marriage. As he moved away from being his mother's "boyfriend," this freed his mother to begin dating again. She met a man and scheduled her wedding a few months before the patient himself married. His mother might never have had the opportunity to remarry without the patient's psychotherapy.

As patients establish a separate, independent self, they realize the ways in which they have been invited to take advantage of their parents. They begin to treat their mothers and fathers more fairly.

Ilena moved away from her parents. She saw the extent to which she had been letting her mother pay the rent, cook the meals, baby-sit for her younger child, and do the laundry for her. She came to see that her mother was tired and too old to do so much work. Now that Ilena was more independent, she took on many of these tasks herself and began to pay her mother for baby-sitting.

Unfortunately, but rarely, there are a few examples in which parents make the existential decision to let their lives worsen. There are cases in which parents continue to pour all of their energy into letting their lives run downhill as a way of attempting beyond reason to reclaim their children's lives. It is more difficult for the offspring to continue to grow toward independence under these circumstances. However, many patients have succeeded.

PATIENTS' TEMPORARY WISH TO CONFRONT OR ABANDON THE PARENTS

There is usually a period of time, while working through the anger, when patients contemplate cutting off their relationship with their parents permanently. It is advisable for therapists to dissuade patients from doing this, because the ties to family are deep and meaningful. During this stage, therapists should caution patients not to make a premature decision until all the working through is completed. Sometimes it seems appropriate to support a temporary separation from family when the patients' anger is so strong that these feelings may be destructive to their parents. However, patients retain the right to choose what relationship, if any, they will maintain with their family. There are occasionally patients for whom the cost of maintaining contact with an enmeshed family may be too high.

The patients and the therapist must wade through the patients' acting out and bring the rage, disappointment, and pain to the surface where it may be used constructively. In the working-through phase, the therapist should try to help patients confine their anger to the psychotherapy hour rather than unload it on their parents. The patients may not be able to resist the temptation to "let the parent have it" in one experimental go-around. This often occurs out of the patients' need to see if they can actually confront their parents. The therapist needs to explain that the parents are not in a position to understand what the patients are attempting to communicate, any more than the patients would have been able to understand in the first hour what the therapist is talking about many hours later. Sometimes the patients and their parents battle it out anyway. Parents react as if they had been thunderstruck. They may retreat in depression and hurt or may be overadaptive, expressing "undying love and concern" for the patients. In some cases, confrontation of this kind may not be excessively harmful because the parents are able to successfully defend against what they are not ready to hear. The patients see, once again, the unwritten rules and the parents' psychological incompleteness. Sadness and empathy begin to replace the anger.

Tom said, "As I watched my wife take on my mother, I was glad that she could finally do it. I felt the anger, too. I also felt a sadness for my mother. She looked so unable to handle the situation. That feeling allowed me to say to my wife, 'Save your breath because Mother is not understanding.' "

This patient was surprised to learn that he can make use of two opposing emotions at the same time. Contradictory feelings no longer need to be split apart. Anger can be used to set constructive limits, and empathy and understanding can be utilized to negotiate the parental relationship instead of totally rejecting it.

Patients may feel a temporary despair when they realize that their parents' psychological incompleteness may not be healed by the patients' new understanding and response. All impinged-upon adults ultimately hope that the psychotherapy will cure not only themselves but their parents as well. In reality, they will still have to continue to handle the demands from their intrapsychic parents. They may also have to manage the manipulations from their real parents by maintaining an awareness of, and acting constructively upon, their own needs and feelings.

PATIENTS REVEAL THE PARENTS' HISTORY

After patients' anger has surfaced and the separation–individuation process is taking place, the patients bring in some information about their grandparents. It is difficult to obtain a full picture of the parents' history because the parents may have said little about the painful or confusing aspects of their own childhood. Usually, however, there are some well-known family legends that contain enough information to let both the patients and the therapists know that the parents have suffered with the same commands that they gave to the patients. These stories are every bit as poignant as the examples given by the patients themselves. When patients can begin to reveal their family history, it becomes possible to deepen respect and understanding for their parents' psychological incompleteness, vulnerability, and suffering.

It is easy to lose track of the parents' competence within their profession or community and talk with patients only about their parents' psychological shortcomings. This becomes a detriment to the therapeutic process because the patients lose track of their parents' actual strengths and lose respect for their parents. When the psychotherapy process is able to acknowledge the parents' assets, the patients eventually come to believe that their parents' ability and capacity for growth can ultimately resolve the symbiotic relationship. The competent side of their parents allows the patients to hope for a new and better relationship.

EXPLAINING TO THE PARENTS

In the process of gaining psychological independence, patients feel very uncomfortable about making changes in their lives without informing and explaining to their parents, because they want to protect themselves from further rejection. They hope that an explanation will help their parents to change in a way that is more gratifying, and they want to protect their special status within the family.

Unfortunately, explaining often accomplishes very little. In fact, more often than not it is detrimental, as is evident in patients' accounts of their discussions to understand separation–individuation issues with their parents. The patients feel a need to test-prove their progress with a successful, rational discussion with their parents. Unfortunately, the parents generally hold up their end of the discussion with skillful sidetracking of any understanding.

These accumulated experiences suggest that the most successful way to tell parents to separate from their children is through consistent action that is the product of working through. Patients take a critical step forward when they can view their parents as fragile and tenacious in their need for psychological support rather than all-powerful. Then the patients can consistently and respectfully resist invitations to continue the enmeshment. The changes in the relationship are delivered behaviorally to the parents through the same channel by which the commands were sent.

PATIENTS RECONNECT WITH THE FAMILY

Many parents have to survive a temporarily difficult period of hostility and rejection from patients during part of the psychotherapy. Parents not only feel the loss of usual contact, but also psychological incompleteness at the absence of their children as extended selves.

Parents tend to respond to the patients' wish for greater independence and separateness in characteristic ways well known to therapists but confusing for patients. For instance, when patients return home to visit, their parents may well have scheduled so many engagements that there is no time to be with the patients. Perhaps it is their way of saying "If you can go away, I can too" or "I can survive without you" (an important message, even if stated childishly through acting out). Patients may feel confused and hurt by this new behavior. The parents may maintain their busy schedule as long as the patients respond with hurt. However, if the patients can understand and take it in stride, the parents may become more available for a more separate relationship.

Parents may also handle the separation by offering a large, enticing gift in apparent but spurious support of a growth step. Perhaps it is their way of saying "I want to be part of the action if you are going to go away, and I want to experiment to see if you will still accept my gift of sabotage." Patients usually feel sorely tempted to accept the gift, especially if it is money, but decide to refuse it. At this point, patients invariably ask, "What kind of relationship is it possible to have with my parents now that I understand who they are and what has happened to me? I can't think how to talk to them. What is there to say?"

All patients long to find a way to go on with life and not leave their parents behind. After all, family is family, and there is no substitute for that. In almost all cases, there is a positive answer.

After this combination of doubt, rejection, and counterrejection has run its course, the parents are ready to end the era of disturbed interaction. They may be so happy about resumed contact that they accept the relationship on new terms. The patients visit without an ax-to-grind because they have come to terms with the fact that their parents are unlikely to meet their needs any more now than in the past. It is ironic that once patients stop asking for love their parents cannot give, a better relationship often results.

Experience suggests that the most successful way to introduce a new, more healthy relationship between patients and parents is through consistent action that is the product of working through. Continued nonverbal action, rather than explanation, is the avenue by which the commands were sent to the patients and therefore is a well-known way to communicate to the parents.

The patients quietly sort out the undermining remarks from the rest of their conversation with their parents and then respectfully decline all invitations to continuing enmeshment. With satisfaction, the patients are able to sidestep, ignore, or make light of psychopathological interaction instead of getting sucked into it. They can avoid starting a useless fight over their parents' manipulative complaints about life problems or physical illnesses. A sabotaging comment can frequently be halted by simply saying nothing or by quietly excusing oneself. When patients' reactions are accompanied by real respect and understanding for their parents' psychological frailty, the parents will gradually accept these new limits.

It takes time, sometimes years, for parents to catch on. In the meantime, there is no way around some awkward stumbling, some defensive anger, hurt feelings, worry, blame, guilt, and rejection. In the midst of the separation process, parents often feel helpless and try to blame the psychotherapy; the patients' new behavior is labeled as "sick."

In patients' initial attempts to alter the enmeshed relationship with their parents, the patients may present limits in a harsh and rejecting manner. This is likely because they still view their parents as very powerful. When patients can view their parents as actually fragile psychologically, they can set limits in a more kindly, respectful, and supportive manner that compassionately encourages their parents' expanded abilities to handle psychological independence. As the parents function more successfully within their marriage and in general, the patients celebrate quietly, because the parents will not be ready to be complimented. It takes time for the parents to risk revealing their success in place of advertising their fragility. Therapists need to guide patients through these various stages toward a mature adult relationship.

In the long run, the parents can even feel proud of, and compliment, the patients' new steadiness. They experience their offspring as coming back into the fold, but they accept the fact that this time, it is pretty much on the patients' terms.

Alice was trying out her new ability to set limits with her family. After a considerable period of silence, she was ready to engage with them. She came back to her next therapy hour after a phone call with her family and said, "It really felt good to call them again. It made my day and theirs too, I think. But it was also very hard, and an unusual way to relate to them. I felt like we were both engaged in a fencing match. Both sides put out what we wanted and both sides protected their territory. I'm not used to relating to Mother as another adult instead of just my mother. It will take some getting used to, but now I am ready to try. I wanted to explain things to them, but I forced myself not to do that because I knew that it wouldn't work."

When patients become assured that nonverbal reactions are effective, they are no longer so fearful of a relationship with family members. The patients do not have to avoid or dread every minute of a family gathering. The parents, in turn, become more responsive when they sense that the anger toward them has dissipated. The time together is often cordial, mildly nurturing, and even fun.

This new contact is less frequent, more superficial, and oriented toward the nonpathological needs of the parents. In-depth conversations about the psychological dynamics of the family usually remain off limits. This becomes acceptable to patients because they have had the therapeutic relationship in which to address such thoughts. Instead, many patients are able to do small things to support their parents' independent growth and achieve some satisfaction from that. When the parents are convinced that they need no longer effectively sabotage their children, they usually begin to see their children's growth steps as useful to them because they can finally feel like proud parents. They are still regarding their children as an extension of themselves, but the sabotage is attenuated.

The following analogy has helped patients understand how their relationship with their parents has changed. When the patient withdraws his or her availability as an extension of the parent, it is as if the parent has a broken leg and must hop or use crutches. The resultant hopping is annoying, since trips together are decidedly limited and slowed down. The parent keeps asking the patient to be a new leg. The patient can decline to do that without knocking the parent over or refusing to visit. Time together can be limited in length and restricted to the kind of activity suitable for a broken leg. However, the parent will never be able to climb hills to see the patient's accomplishments. The patient and parent may have to live with the parent's broken leg because the parent may not choose to, or feel capable of, fixing it. That does not mean that the patient has to fix it for the parent; the patient is only responsible for repairing his or her own incomplete self.

As the relationships with family members improve, patients will want to respond with a loving gesture. It is easy to forget command 9 (I will reject any offer of intimacy or love. I am not interested in understanding the difference between symbiosis and intimacy).

Martha bought her mother a lovely Christmas present. She wanted her mother to enjoy it. Her mother called to thank her but seemed withdrawn and distant. She spoke without pleasure about the gift and preferred to talk about the wrapping paper and presents she had bought for another sibling who was experiencing financial difficulty. Martha had probably acted too competently and made her mother feel uneasy. She would have done better, in terms of her relationship with her mother, to buy a present of lesser quality. However, Martha's understanding of why her mother withdrew helped her not to feel hurt. Several months later, her father reported that "Mother really enjoyed the gift."

Everyone feels relief as the patients restore a relationship with their families. The patients, and the parents too, feel some sense of sadness at the hours spent feeling hostile and apart while working to understand and gain the necessary freedom. This sadness can serve as a signal to help both parties realize that they are willing to work to keep their relationship with each other.

There are moments in psychotherapy that make all the work worthwhile for therapists. One is seeing a patient reclaim and use a feeling previously forbidden by the commands. Another is hearing about a successful family gathering in which both the patient and the parents enjoyed themselves.

PATIENTS LEARN TO LOVE AND TO BUILD THEIR OWN FAMILIES

As impinged-upon adults achieve independence and begin to feel their own separate selves, they want to try out their ability to be loving. A pet can be a useful adjunct to the psychotherapy at this point.

Arleen learned that she could have a baby without necessarily repeating the enmeshment that had happened within her own family. However, she needed to test out her ability to be an appropriate caretaker first. She bought a puppy and began her relationship with the dog by feeding and grooming it, training it, and caring for it through a severe illness. During this time she received several sabotaging letters from her family. She felt confused about her ability to lovingly care for the dog. Her confusion was expressed when she brought the dog in her car to her therapy hour. She wanted me to see that the dog was alive and healthy. I invited the dog into the therapy hour. Arleen declined, fearing damage to my office, but remembered the invitation as a statement of confidence in her ability to be a nurturing parent. The dog was a pilot study. Arleen went on with her psychotherapy and was eventually able to have her own baby.

Andy accepted his therapist's suggestion that he buy a dog when he moved into his own apartment in the city and felt the need for protection and company. He bought a puppy and brought her to a therapy hour. I went outside to see the dog during the last five minutes of the hour and was openly affectionate with the animal, letting the dog lick my face. Andy was surprised. In the following hour, he revealed that he was unable to let the dog touch him above the waist. He was afraid that the expressed love from the dog would be intrusive.

Gradually he was able to let the dog into his life. He went on a vacation and decided to put the dog in a kennel where the animal would be "sure to be safe." He cried when he left the dog, and the dog was "ecstatic" to see him when he returned. The two of them had managed loving and separation.

Once Andy felt competent to love, he was able to have a girlfriend. They lived together and later married.

CONCLUSION

Although the patient's extended family rarely seeks psychotherapy, therapists should always keep them in mind and hope that the work done by patients and therapists will eventually have beneficial results for the rest of the patient's family. Occasionally, I hear about a family that seems to have made outstanding progress apparently merely by being the recipient of a patient's behavioral changes.

As a result of Mary's psychotherapy, her sister stopped being suicidal and ceased calling her every week. Her mother no longer assumed full responsibility for the care of Mary's grandmother who, in turn, was able to buy her own food and clothes for the first time in forty years. Mary's mother returned to school. Her brother fell in love despite family disapproval. Mary's father and mother became more affectionate with each other and even flaunted their renewed marriage.

Of course there is no mathematical proof that all this resulted from Mary's therapeutic experience, but Mary was aware of no other variable producing the changes. When this happens, it is the final lesson for patients. Enmeshment activities are destructive not only to the patient but to each of the family participants.

CHAPTER 6

Commands Given by Impinged-upon Adults to Friends, Peers, and Colleagues

The commands from mothers and fathers and their painful consequences have already been considered in this book. But there is more to understand before it is possible to accomplish the birth of a self. This chapter examines the way in which impinged-upon adults try to compensate for their incompleteness by developing their own set of commands to give to other people.

Impinged-upon adult patients may be nurses, lawyers, poets, writers, musicians, psychologists, pharmacists, researchers, and scientists, and some may be parents. Many have managed to enter a profession but remain burdened with a sense of confusion and guilt. They are aware of their talent, on the one hand, but on the other, they feel insecure, guilty, and angry about their lack of support for success.

Betty was in the last month of her pregnancy and was preparing for delivery by going to Lamaze classes.

Betty: I saw some films of deliveries and found myself crying. It was not just tears running down my face. I just wanted to sob. I couldn't figure out what was happening to me. I was so surprised.

Therapist: Can you return to that feeling now?

Betty: (She thought for a while, as I watched her face slowly cloud with emotion.) Well, it was the baby. It hadn't done anything, yet it was getting so much pride and support and love from the parents. I just couldn't believe it.

Therapist: And you've worked so hard for the same kind of support from your parents.

Betty: I tried to imagine how my parents would look in such a film when I was born. I suppose they were very proud then too. But so soon the pride stopped. My father must have been proud because, all the way up through my adolescence, he used to call me "My little baby."

Therapist: He just couldn't acknowledge that you had changed into anything else.

Betty: If he saw me now, he'd still say the same thing. He doesn't know anything about my creative abilities, my degree, my marriage.

Therapist: What are you feeling now?

Betty: Just so sad. . . .

Therapist: So the film brought up deep feelings of loss about your lack of support.

Having spent a good part of their lives being extensions of their parents and lacking a sense of being whole persons, impinged-upon adults turn to others with a set of commands that require others to provide what is lacking. Many of the commands in this chapter have been created by impinged-upon adults to get the kind of validation for their success that they felt deprived of in childhood.

Some patients feel as if they had no real friends at all. Others feel difficulty in maintaining friendships, an issue to be considered further in the following chapter. This difficulty in finding friends is puzzling because they feel that they have given more than they get back in relationships, especially with family.

Sometimes, adult patients can find a friend who has complementary psychological needs. Then they mutually obey each other's commands. This system may work quite well for a time. Then, for some reason, one partner fails to obey a command. Rejection can happen with sufficient swiftness to disrupt or break off the relationship without warning or discussion. Since this may have happened repeatedly, impinged-upon adults are sensitive and alert to this possibility, thus making it hard for them to trust in other people.

The following vignette expresses the doubt and anxiety that many impinged-upon adults feel in relationships with other people.

Donna came to her third hour on time. I was about three minutes late coming into the waiting room to get her. Donna became anxious. After about two minutes, she left the waiting room to come into my office and asked whether I knew that she was there. I replied assuringly, "I heard you come in and will be with you directly." As I ushered her into the office, Donna mumbled with embarrassment, "I don't know the rules yet."

My response to her was that she had not violated any rule, but suggested that we take some time to talk about her feelings.

This simple event became the subject for Donna's entire third hour. First, we discussed the myth of perfection. Someone was not perfect. Perhaps it was me (the therapist) because I was late. If I was not perfect, maybe I was not the right therapist. Perhaps Donna should leave. However, if Donna could help me to rectify my mistake quickly, then I might qualify to remain as her therapist. Donna also felt a responsibility to take care of me. Perhaps I had not heard her enter the office. On the other hand, perhaps Donna was the one who was not perfect because she had not learned the "unwritten rules" of the office (the commands within any relationship). Therefore, Donna deserved to miss part of her hour, or, if she was not perfect, perhaps I was rejecting her already. Since Donna's thoughts and feelings had seemed unimportant to her parents, perhaps I too had forgotten her work.

The possibility that Donna had not considered was the actual reason for my lateness.

I explained, "I am usually able to be on time. Today I needed to be a little late for your hour because I wanted to review a portion of the notes I had taken during your initial evaluation. I also needed a few minutes of rest after the previous hour, which was a difficult one. Sometimes I might be a few minutes late to ensure that when I see you I am prepared and in a position to give you my full attention. I will always make up any lateness at the end of the hour."

Donna was surprised that my "imperfection" was on her behalf.

The following commands represent patients' attempts to provide unwritten rules of their own that will make their relationships feel more secure. Each of the psychopathological commands in this chapter, and its corresponding permission, represent the ends of a continuum along which most people fall. Many, if not most, people use some of these rules with other people some of the time. Therapists need to be familiar with these commands and careful not to give them to patients as a way of healing the therapists' own personal sense of incompleteness.

SEVEN PATIENT COMMANDS AND THEIR CORRESPONDING PERMISSIONS

COMMAND 1

I will listen to what you want and give it, with the obligation that you are to like my gift and give one back to me, which will provide me with the feeling that I exist.

Many patients give gifts. In fact, they can be counted on to remember others with presents at the time of traditional holidays and birthday celebrations. It may be painful or nearly impossible for these patients to simply receive a gift. Instead, the patients feel a strong obligation to reciprocate because they feel compelled to keep up the symbiotic giving and taking that maintains psychological equilibrium. They also feel obligated to like the gift they have received.

Some patients want to give gifts with specific directions: a handmade plant basket should be displayed in a specific location in the therapist's office. If therapists comply, the patients feel special because the gift holds a prized place. If therapists feel pulled to respond to a gift in a particular way, then it is likely a gift with a command.

Therapists have tried to avoid this issue by making rules: Robert Langs (1973) advises therapists never to accept a gift and warns that to do so will always be collusive. It does not seem necessary to take this position under all circumstances. There are times when accepting a gift is therapeutic. However, when the gift comes with an obligation, as in command 1, it needs to be talked through.

Althea gave her new boyfriend five Christmas presents. She entered my office in considerable psychological and psychosomatic pain because her boyfriend had responded with attack and rejection. As she and I explored the matter further, it became evident that these "gifts" were not freely given as an expression of loving him. Instead, they were her efforts to do what she thought he wanted. In return, he was to respond in kind, making her feel appreciated and loved. She was feeling especially unlovable because the psychotherapeutic process was allowing her to see the reality of her parents' unavailability. The presents were not a gift but an obligation. Her boyfriend felt overwhelmed, called her "controlling" and requested an end to the relationship. Althea despaired. From her perspective, she had given to her parents and not gotten what she needed in terms of love and support for growth. She felt valueless, because she had to give too much to get anything back. When she gave extra to her boyfriend, he withdrew, increasing her feelings of worthlessness.

When Althea and I talked about the difference between command 1 and real giving, she replied, "I don't think that I know what giving is." From her perspective, it was a difficult concept to understand. The corresponding permission for a psychologically healthy person helped me to explore the difference with her.

PERMISSION 1

I will listen to what you want and will give it, as long as it does not compromise me too much. You are under no obligation to like my gift or to give one back to me.

A gift is given freely as an expression of affection. The person who receives it is free to enjoy it or give it away if it is not suitable. The receiver can decide what to do with the gift without worrying about the consequences to the relationship.

Underlying all the healthy permissions is the following premise:

I know that I exist as a whole and unique person. I believe that we can be friends if that is your wish.

COMMAND 2

If I know something that you don't know, you should listen to me so that I feel validated. We will then share the same knowledge, so that we feel at one with each other.

This command is especially important for highly intelligent or creative patients with separation problems, who also have a natural wish to acquire skill and share their expertise with others. Such patients seek out opportunities to teach others or be center stage as a way of achieving recognition. These patients tend to feel defensive, unsure, and tense because of their conflict about growth. This may result in a kind of reaction–formation that makes them come on too strong or be controlling, domineering, or condescending toward others who lack the same capability.

Alice shared a new method of teaching mathematics with fellow teachers in an afterschool seminar. She had researched the matter carefully and was well prepared. Instead of engaging her audience in a discussion, she lectured in a manner that displayed her expertise. Her audience was very quiet. She was disappointed that they did not ask questions or praise her for her presentation. In fact, the audience probably felt no chance to share their own ideas and thoughts and felt an uncomfortable obligation to provide validation.

The corresponding permission allowing for more healthy interaction is as follows:

PERMISSION 2

If I know something that you don't know, I will share it with you, provided that you express an interest. You are under no obligation to agree with me or to remember it. Perhaps you will share something I don't know in exchange.

COMMAND 3

I will invite you into my home with the obligation that you then invite me to your home. That way, I will feel liked and will be able to display to the world that I am worthy of friends.

Impinged-upon adults generally have friendships, but friends are often secondary to the maintenance of self-esteem. Many patients dread being alone because it feels as if no one wants to be with them. They want to have an active social calendar not only because it is fun to do things with other people but because they need to feel worthy of friends. The fuller the social calendar, the better they feel about themselves. They also feel a strong pressure to reciprocate every social situation to which they have been invited so that no symbiotic relationships will be disrupted. Depression often results if they are left out of any social event.

Impinged-upon adults are uncomfortable having a friend visit unless their home is orderly and complete. A new friend may be postponed for several months because remodeling has not been finished or wallpaper is not hung in the dining room. Impinged-upon adults feel uneasy if their house is not perfect because their new friend may evaluate it negatively and never reciprocate.

Tina said as if there were never any question about the matter, "When my child begins to walk, I will have to put away all of my valuable things. I just won't have any company until he is older and I can put the things back."

The corresponding permission implies a much greater sense of flexibility and freedom:

PERMISSION 3

I will invite you into my home as a statement of my wish to be open with you and to offer you something. You are under no obligation to like my home or to invite me to yours. I would like to see your home as a statement of who you are.

COMMAND 4

I may master many tasks, and you must constantly be on call to observe my work, to evaluate it for me, and to give me praise and support in place of the sabotage given by my parents. I cannot believe in the worth of anything I do, even though I know it is good, unless you like it too. You may keep me company by doing some of the same tasks, but I feel more secure if I can do them better.

Anyone can lose perspective on a project when working closely on it for a long time. Everyone needs feedback and validation, but the problem of impinged-upon adults is more pressing than this natural need for support. Command 4 is meant to relieve impinged-upon adults' constant feeling of insecurity about the value of their accomplishments. Their own positive value judgments about their work were lost in childhood in their interactions with their parents. Impinged-upon adults maintain a sense of self-worth by checking with others for validation.

In addition, impinged-upon adults may have a stronger need to do the best work rather than to share the accomplishment and praise with others. The myth of self-righteous perfection drives them to strive too hard, failing to recognize progress.

Frank was doing very well as a writer. In fact, he had good reason to believe that he was one of the best writers in his class. His teacher became ill and was not available to teach the class for a time. Without the teacher's constant positive feedback, Frank began to experience "writer's block," during which time he was unable to produce any work.

Jim, a dentist, felt very uncomfortable when a new dentist was hired to come into his office, and he overheard the boss talking about the competence of this new employee. He felt that he should offer to resign, because he might not be "the best" any longer. He lost sight of the value of his own work. Later, Jim understood that he wanted to hold the same place at work that he thought he had in the family. At home, he felt "special," "best," "perfect," and "protected," as long as he obeyed the commands better than his siblings. If he was not "best" in the office, he was afraid of being abandoned. He was fearful to undertake certain new dental procedures for fear of making a mistake.

Don was a social worker and liked to have other social workers to his home for dinner. Invariably, he would start a conversation in which he disclosed something of a personal nature. His wife became uncomfortable with his personal revelations and often found an excuse to leave the room. He would gain the attention of most of the people in the room and would feel validated by them. He realized that he was seeking the kind of special attention he used to get at home, but at the cost of violating his own privacy.

It is a significant moment when patients are able to appreciate the value of the hard work they do in therapy without direct validation from the therapist. They feel a more whole sense of self.

The psychologically healthy permission provides another perspective:

PERMISSION 4

I may master many tasks. I will evaluate my work myself. If you are interested, I will elicit your feedback to enhance the quality of my work. I will encourage you to master what you wish, even if it turns out to be a task that is greater than mine. I may feel jealous, but I will use that feeling to organize a new challenge for myself rather than to sabotage you. We can share our work and learn from each other. I will never take credit for what you have done yourself.

This permission points out a comfortable separateness. Each person is able to share and even be enhanced by the other's work, while the boundaries and credit for work remain separate. Envy and jealousy are not bad words to be suppressed. The feeling of competition is minimized because there is room for two separate people to be competent at the same time. Patients can thus feel encouraged to achieve success because there is no threat of abandonment.

Donna described her husband as "selfish" because he had a strong commitment to a career that took him away from his wife and child half of each day. She had learned to use the word selfish from her parents in place of the words "professional dedication or motivation." I suggested that perhaps she felt left out, envious, or jealous because of his occupational accomplishments. She felt embarrassed that I exposed these feelings because she had been taught that envy and jealousy were bad. She had never viewed these feelings as indications that she, too, wanted a career that would bring her a sense of mastery while her husband was working. She had contented herself with being merely an extension of his career by helping with his profession. It had not occurred to her to take credit for the help she had given and to recognize her talent for her own career.

COMMAND 5

You must accept my being condescending to or angry with you because I need to transfer my feelings about my parents onto you.

Some impinged-upon adults hide their feelings of confusion about who they are and what they have to offer by being condescending to those "who can't manage worth a damn anyway." Sometimes it feels easier to look down on the world as a defense against admitting disappointment with and confusion about important past relationships.

Therefore, the attitude of impinged-upon adults may seem unfriendly. Other people may respond with feelings of inferiority and withdrawal. Impinged-upon adults' condescension is their way of signaling the following feelings:

"Something went wrong for me with my parents. My parents ought to have known better. Even a kid understands that something went wrong. I am not as bad as I am made out to be. . . . You are worse than I am."

This attitude tends to be characteristic of patients who are exceptionally creative or talented. They have a hard time being patient with people less able than themselves and perceive them as barriers to growth. Impinged-upon adults may rise quickly into management positions because of their talent and then run into difficulty as a leader because of their proclivity to be condescending.

On the other hand, impinged-upon adults are afraid to provide constructive criticism to others because they were punished for disagreeing with their parents. They also fearfully perceive that any expression of negative feelings provides an opportunity for their anger to surface. Therefore they try to control their feelings, only to have this emotion slip out in the guise of condescension or sarcasm.

Condescension also represents the patients' attempt to explain their resentment at the imbalance between giving and receiving support in relation to the family. As one patient explained,

I guess I decided that since I had to do all the reaching out, I must be better than my family and other people who just wait around to receive all I do for them.

A cycle develops in which patients feel the lack of reciprocal support and then become more condescending, which results in feeling more and more left out. The attitude of condescension may emerge whenever a peer or mentor stops being supportive. The other person is then viewed as suddenly acting like the parents. Therapists can break into this cycle with a proper understanding of what impinged-upon adults are trying to communicate.

The corresponding permission is as follows:

PERMISSION 5

Sometimes I may be condescending or rude in some way toward you because I do not understand some feeling within myself. I hope that you will confront me so that I can notice what I don't understand.

COMMAND 6

I will listen intently to what you need and will be very good to you. In return, you must tell the world what a fine person I am.

Impinged-upon adult patients know when the therapist's mind wanders even for a moment and when the therapist glances at the clock. The patients will often stop and ask, "Do you understand what I mean?" or subtly shift the topic to reengage the therapist. This perceptive ability can be put to use trying to do the right thing for other people, so that, in turn, someone will say, "You are a fine person." The issue is again the search for a perfection that will finally bring love from the family.

Concomitantly, impinged-upon adults do many things because they do care about other people. But it is a big moment when they can feel secure enough about their own sense of self to be good to someone else just as a statement of their growing ability to be intimate. The two interactions feel different.

It is difficult to give an example of this command because it is internal and rarely admitted by patients. Others interacting with these patients may feel the ulterior motive in the background. This command is usually carried into adult life as a habitual way of trying to resolve the question, "Why do my parents give me so little credit or praise for all the things I do for them?"

The psychologically healthy permission is as follows:

PERMISSION 6

I will be good to you as a statement of my caring about our relationship. If you are not good to me, I will ask you about it to protect our relationship. I will not let you abuse me because that would not be good for either of us.

When impinged-upon adults become self-sustaining persons, constructive interaction comes automatically.

Toward the end of his therapy Dan said, "Now I would like to contribute something important and meaningful during the course of my lifetime. I am in the process of figuring out just what it will be." He was excited and not concerned about whether others would think he was a fine person. He valued himself.

COMMAND 7

I depend on your daily responses to make me feel like a whole person. If you disobey, I will be mad. I will see you as a bad person, while I will try to feel like the good person. Even if you obey all these commands, I will continue to need your help. If you keep obeying, you will rescue me from ever becoming a whole, self-evaluating person. In the meantime, we can't truly be friends; we can only need each other.

Many impinged-upon adults recognize that psychological survival would be extremely difficult for them in situations where they were forced to be alone. They know intuitively that they need the approval of others to validate their existence. As long as they are in need of this constant kind of support, their friends feel pressured to act in a particular way toward them. Their friends are damned if they do and damned if they don't in terms of contributing to the relationship. If the enmeshed support is supplied, the relationship remains symbiotic. If it is refused, the relationship may be lost through rejection.

Regarding the relationship with his girl friend, Bob said, "I need her to come and visit me in my office at least once a day. I do fantastic work for her because I need her to tell me it's wonderful. When she comes to see me, I experience a high; her presence is like a fix. If she doesn't come, it feels like the bottom dropped out. When she withdraws her attention, I can be very cold to her. It is an addictive relationship that feels great when she is there, but too painful when she is not."

PERMISSION 7

I will try not to use your responses to me as proof that I am a valued person. If you are unresponsive to me, I will ask why. You might be troubled about something in your own life or I might be doing something that turns you off. I want to clarify the difference so that I can give you support for your trouble or change my response, as needed.

Society does not give people much encouragement to use this permission. Instead, they are taught to be polite to each other in ways that ignore their ability to notice when someone else is upset, much less to ask about it. Communication is badly compromised because people are afraid to admit to negative feelings and to help each other through them.

In utilizing the commands, patients must present a truly compromised version of their real self to others. Anyone who will validate the patients' self will be accepted into a relationship without much discrimination. Patients, therefore, may acquire friends with their own limited set of commands. Real thoughts and feelings are put aside to exchange validations and commands. As these friendships lengthen, so do the resentments that are a natural outgrowth of real feelings, and are never addressed. The patient's lack of contact with his own self makes it all the more necessary to validate his existence in and through the eyes of others.

How do patients come to realize all of this and attempt to change, and how is it even possible? Sometimes the issue comes into focus when patients complete a creative project that is a part of their real self and realize that they are terrified to introduce it to the real world. Sometimes it starts when patients decide to express their true feelings within one important relationship. The feelings may be expressed too strongly or awkwardly because the patients are so out of practice. The friend may be hurt or unable to understand, or the friend's commands may be broken. The relationship is seriously disrupted and perhaps even lost.

The patients may then find themselves left alone. There is an existential decision to make at this point: whether to repair the relationship by taking back their real thoughts and feelings or putting away the creative project, or to let the real self step out into the world and risk another loss. The patients feel knocked back and are easily convinced to return to the former mode.

Patients have to allow their real self to emerge by abandoning the commands and taking on the responsibility of validation by succeeding in doing what is best for them. Patients may need to leave behind some old friendships and endure the loneliness until new, more healthy ones are started.

Patients have to make a new discrimination. As impinged-upon adults, they have been taught that doing what is best for others feels good and reduces anxiety. Doing what is best for themselves also feels good but increases anxiety. There is a subtle difference between the two kinds of "feeling good"; the patients learn the difference. They learn to defer less to others and to negotiate more honestly and constructively, instead of wielding the commands manipulatively.

If patients try to venture this far, they will begin to notice the numerous times a day they defer to others' needs. The emergence of their real self slowly becomes more important than the number of friends they have. Some relationships may move into the background to become casual acquaintances, while a friend or two who can support and understand the patients' changes will be brought forward into the future. The patients leave behind validation from others and risk loss and failure with the knowledge that they are proud of their mastery of their forward journey. They find that they have a more genuine self to give to others because resentments are fading and manipulative giving is reduced.

For some, this last journey is too steep a climb; for others, it takes years and years. For some, a new self emerges rapidly as a consequence of a trauma or crisis, and as a result of the existential decision to change. What is left of the intrapsychic pathological parents may make this last journey a miserable one filled with doubt, fear, psychosomatic symptoms, depression, and fatigue. The patients must fight constantly with an exhausting labor that pushes forth a new, real self with faults and weaknesses. There are enough people in the external world who will support the patient's journey. Therapists' objectivity and constant support for this new self is a critical ingredient.

CHAPTER 7

Impinged-upon Adults' Relationships with Others

THE ROLE OF CONSTANT ANXIETY

Anxiety is a universal symptom, and a reliable and appropriate signal, occurring when a person approaches an unfamiliar or dangerous situation. However, for impinged-upon adults, anxiety tends to be ever-present, with varying degrees of intensity (Masterson 1983).

Some impinged-upon adults may evidence a variety of forms of anxiety attacks. The physiological event occurs when their anxiety is very intense but as such is out of the patients' conscious awareness. The most common physical response is dizziness, which may be accompanied by shortness of breath; another is chest pains, heart palpitations, or both, and some pain or numbness in a limb, as occurs in a heart attack. An additional response may be a feeling of detachment. Patients describe this feeling with such statements as

I seem to need to protect myself somehow by the feeling that I have stepped out of myself and the interaction. I am floating off somewhere else, looking down at whatever is going on. I am disconnected from my feelings.

Some of these symptoms are exacerbated by hyperventilation.* However, patients are unaware of breathing improperly until the physical symptoms manifest themselves. When hyperventilation-related symptoms are identified during the psychotherapy hour, the patients can be directed to sit back, relax, and cup their hands over their mouth and nose, breathing deeply and regularly to restore the proper balance of carbon dioxide and oxygen in their body.

Although most patients tend to report anxiety in the form of mild dizziness, some have had attacks so severe that it suddenly throws them to the ground or knocks something they are holding out of their hand. The first attack, especially if severe, can be very frightening because the patients fear a malfunction in their brain or heart. The emergency room diagnosis is usually psychosomatic.

When patients then seek the aid of a psychotherapist, it is often possible to determine why the attack occurred. The patients have usually taken a major step forward with life or may be trying to relax by taking a vacation and fear parental abandonment. None of these feelings reach a conscious level but manifest themselves instead in the form of a physiological "attack."

Even after a complete medical workup, patients usually need time to be convinced that the symptom does not have an organic basis. The belief that something is physically wrong is a powerful defense against facing the psychological conflict. Once patients become convinced that it is their anxiety that is being expressed psychosomatically, the attacks may diminish in severity and frequency because the patients are no longer afraid of a heart attack or a brain tumor.

PSYCHOSOMATIC SYMPTOMS

There are other psychosomatic symptoms that bring impinged-upon adults into psychotherapy. One of these is asthma-like. For some patients, it tends to be different from the usual form of asthma in which a person experiences difficulty breathing out.

---

*Anxious persons develop the feeling of not being able to get enough air, producing the feeling of constriction and chest pain, which leads to further overbreathing. They fail to rebreathe enough carbon dioxide, present in exhaled air. The lower level of blood carbon dioxide produces symptoms of numbness, tingling of the hands, and dizziness.

Many patients struggle to breathe in, describing a shortness of breath. Perhaps this kind of asthma accurately portrays their difficulty with taking in "fresh air" in the larger world. For example, mild asthma may start when the therapist gives a new interpretation to the patient.

A second symptom is a runny nose, which patients tend to call "my allergies." Frequently the runny nose starts about three hours before a therapy hour. If patient and therapist are able to understand the issue correctly during the session, the runny nose will often dry up completely. Sometimes nasal congestion begins during the therapy hour in response to an issue that has been raised and ceases as soon as patients have fully expressed their feelings regarding this issue.

A third psychosomatic symptom is itching. An irritated area, when scratched, soon develops into a small white welt. If the itching becomes more intense, and patients continue to scratch, the number of welts increases. This most often occurs in areas on the inside of the legs and arms or behind the ears. One patient could guarantee that she would experience itching as soon as she started talking to her mother on the telephone. The itching diminished rapidly after the conversation ended. Sometimes it occurs during a psychotherapy hour.

Much more difficult to describe is a generalized aching physical discomfort relieved only by changing position. It is the restless feeling that accompanies being restrained or having limited freedom of movement. This symptom can be acutely uncomfortable and generally occurs in the area of the abdomen extending sometimes to the calf muscles of the legs and lower arms.

Therapists of impinged-upon adults may also experience any of these symptoms during a patient hour as a countertransference response to their patients' material.

These psychosomatic symptoms can provide useful information when they occur during a psychotherapy session. Therefore, therapists should suggest to their patients that they interrupt whatever they and the therapists are talking about so that the patients can tell the therapists when an attack is happening; this warning gives patients and therapists the opportunity to translate important unconscious feelings into communication. Sometimes the reason for the symptoms remains obscure, but often the symptom signals a painful feeling or memory that has been unconscious.

It is fairly common for patients to report that psychosomatic symptoms occur periodically in between psychotherapy hours. While the therapeutic work continues, patients learn to manage their lives in spite of these psychosomatic occurrences and realize that others rarely know when an attack is happening. One patient learned to continue to drive his motorcycle safely during anxiety attacks. If the symptoms are severe, it is advisable that patients consult a physician for medication to minimize the discomfort. After patients get beyond the fear of being abandoned and resolve the separation conflict, anxiety symptoms usually disappear completely. The absence of attacks is one of the many reliable signs that the psychotherapy is satisfactorily progressing or completed.

It is impressive to note the courage with which impinged-upon adults accept, manage, interpret, and conquer these discomforts as a part of the psychotherapy process.

THE STANCE OR POSTURE OF IMPINGED-UPON ADULTS

Some impinged-upon adults will complain of poor posture. Stooping slightly or rounding the shoulders are ways to look nonthreatening; women may assume this posture to underemphasize their breasts, signs of maturity or sexuality. Others may adopt a slightly awkward gait, such as a mild limp; in this way, impinged-upon adults manage to get around, but still look injured or in need of help from their parents. This posture and movement also seem to be unconscious and deeply ingrained habits that demonstrate the degree to which impinged-upon adults feel weighed down by the commands.

This posture disguises creativity and maturity, limits smooth spontaneous movement, and indicates that the patients are unhappy (depressed). Finally, some patients, in a retaliative and defiant way, develop a way of walking and moving that advertises just how much they feel "ruined or damaged" by their parental relationships.

RELATIONSHIPS WITH OTHERS FEEL UNEQUAL

Patients express some dissatisfactions in common about their relationships with others. They complain that once they have established a friendship, they feel a greater obligation to be the one to maintain the relationship. If they call up friends and initiate plans to get together, everything seems fine. The friends may indicate that they are having a good time. Nonetheless, if the patients don't call their friends, they have the feeling that their friends will abandon them by never calling back.

The patients feel that something is wrong. If they try to talk about the complication, their friends appear unable to respond, may get upset, and may sometimes cut off the relationship. The patients perceive other people's friendships as having more give and take, and feel inadequate and shy. There are a number of different reasons why this might be occurring.

First, impinged-upon adults may unconsciously attract people who need to be taken care of in an enmeshed way. After all, this is the kind of relationship they are used to. Impinged-upon adults may be putting considerable strain on their relationships because they need their friends to validate them in a way that their parents did not.

Sometimes friends are asked, rather shyly by patients, to show up for an event such as a graduation, or theater or concert performance, in effect to be supportive as a substitute for the patients' parents. The friends do not realize the importance to the patients of supporting this occasion and may treat the event "too casually." The patients feel unsupported once again.

Patients frequently displace feelings of abandonment and rejection from their parents onto their friends. This happens because the patients are oversensitive to feeling disliked and in turn may retreat prematurely.

Finally, the patients, as children, received their self-esteem from hearing their parents say "You are the most perfect person I have ever met" when the commands were obeyed. The patients therefore never got to decide what they felt about themselves; as adults, they continue just to comply, hoping to get the love and respect they deserve. They feel confused and turn to friends for clarification, validation, and self-esteem. Friends may feel that something more is wanted than a friendship. As one friend of a patient said, "I feel as if I am supposed to be doing something for you and I don't know what it is. I'm afraid I am not doing it right. I feel like I am walking on eggshells with you."

PATIENTS' REEVALUATION OF THEIR RELATIONSHIPS

During the course of psychotherapy, patients have to understand the difference between an enmeshed, or symbiotic, relationship and a healthy one. The patients have been exploited by, or have been exploiting, others in the service of psychological incompleteness and unresolved self-esteem. It is discouraging to learn that current relationships may be modeled after the one that patients had with their parents and are in need of change. Gradually patients learn to tell the difference and can sometimes detect the potential for a new, enmeshed relationship because, as one patient said, "it happens like two magnets pulled together. We meet and feel too much like fond friends by the end of a short meeting. We click immediately."

Patients learn that a real friendship develops slowly and carefully, out of the sharing of feelings over time with tolerance and freedom for each person to make mistakes and to come and go within the relationship.

PATIENTS' CONFUSING PRESENTATION
   OF THEIR CAPABILITIES

Impinged-upon adults often unconsciously interfere with the way they present their true intellectual ability. They work hard and do very well in school, appearing on honor rolls and in honor societies. However, they experience difficulty on the aptitude and achievement tests required throughout the educational process. Sometimes this unfortunate phenomenon fails to show itself until patients attempt their final qualifying or licensing examination in the course of career development. Patients become genuinely confused about their actual level of intelligence and do not know what to do about it. Are they retarded, they wonder, because they flunk achievement tests, despite the capabilities that earned them straight A's?

Laurie's parents wanted her to attend a private school. Her grade point average was high. She took the Scholastic Aptitude Test several times but always achieved scores that were twenty points below the level required for entrance into such selective schools. Her scores puzzled counselors and teachers, and Laurie was humiliated by this embarrassing discrepancy in her performance. She never even qualified for an entrance interview.

Paula did extremely well in all but one of her college classes each semester. In that class she would "space out," fail to listen, and feel as if she couldn't comprehend the material. She would fail that class and get A's in all the rest of her work. The one poor grade dropped her grade point average too low to apply to the best medical schools. She asked, "Am I a bright student or not?"

These patients are acting out, oblivious to underlying feelings. In therapy, they discover that the "A" student is the real self trying for mastery in the profession of their choice. The failing patient may be subverting his or her growth to avoid parental abandonment. On the other hand, the failure may also be another part of the real self trying, by the only means possible, to block progress toward fulfillment of their parents' demand for high academic achievement. It is a way for the patients to say no to their parents without being overtly disobedient. In fact, the "no" may be said so skillfully that the parents sometimes lose sight of their own selfish need for their child to achieve in a particular way and feel sympathy for the child who is failing academically.

If impinged-upon adults fail all course work or drop out of school, they are probably manifesting the talionic impulse, a more severe and pervasive form of total retaliative resistance, the purpose of which is to punish the impinging, enmeshed parents (Masterson 1981).

PATIENTS' RELATIONSHIPS WITH THEIR OWN CHILDREN

Many patients overcome the command from mothers or fathers that specifically forbids children to start their own family. However, they may doubt their ability to parent their children differently from the way they were parented. They may feel guilty about the anger that emerges when their children do something to block the natural progress of daily activities. They learn that this anger is transferred from old enmeshed relationships. Sometimes these parents wish their children could be as obedient as they were with their own parents. However, they come to appreciate their children's behavior as natural assertiveness, independence, curiosity, and creativity, instead of resistance or sabotage.

As parents these patients tend to feel unnecessarily guilty about minor mistakes and are genuinely surprised to learn that it is impossible to be perfect parents. They learn to openly express feelings both negative and positive. They begin to consider their children's feelings about a difficult situation, rather than pretending that they have all the answers. They give themselves permission to be angry with their children's negative behavior, but in a constructive, controlled way.

Patients are pleased to learn that they are able to set firm limits with their children as a form of discipline and as a way of encouraging responsibility and mastery. They are used to parents who told them about a rule and then let them break it, who did everything for them, and who frequently let them get away with not doing things they could really do for themselves. With their children they learn to set limits and that these limits are perceived by their children as loving.

THE PRESENTATION OF A CREATIVE SELF

As patients start utilizing their talent and creativity, they discover that it is generally well received for the first time in their lives. They want to allow their creativity to unfold freely and may appear cocky to those who do not understand their history. What is lacking at this point is an ability to be diplomatic in presenting their abilities to others. Sometimes at this juncture they need guidance with the issues of timing and tact. Then it becomes possible to withhold a good idea if co-workers are not yet ready to make use of it.

Sometimes patients discover a talent previously unrecognized. At first they find it difficult to perceive that their performance may be surpassing that of their peers much of the time. Instead of clearly recognizing their talent, they feel confused and get impatient and condescending with those less talented. Co-workers may feel envious, insulted by the patients' impatience, and resent the patients' need for validation. If impinged-upon adults can accept their talent, with all the advantages and disadvantages of such a gift, they can allow their creativity to emerge quietly and let it speak for itself.

THE SEARCH FOR A PARTNER

Many impinged-upon adults come into therapy because they do not feel able to look for and maintain a dating relationship long enough to find a marriage partner. Their goal in psychotherapy is to understand why and to find a mate. Once they have clarified the issues that kept them from dating, they initiate the search for a partner.

Their nonverbal behavior communicates the kind of partner they seek. At first, they may pick someone who is only able to provide a "one-night stand" or a limited friendship. The result is disappointment, but they gain experience and go on. In the process of their experiments, they sometimes question the therapy because they expect the therapist to produce the right partner as part of the "cure." It is not unusual for them to pick an impinged-upon partner who is talented and kind but is also caught up in an enmeshed family and therefore unable to make a full commitment.

Eventually, the patients move on to a more available steady partner. This partner may also have had a history of impingement but has discovered a way to surmount it. They share a similar kind of background and can help each other with the continuing process of separation from family. Sometimes the new partners are in need of psychotherapy to complete a commitment to each other. In such cases, they may come in for conjoint therapy or the partner may be referred to another therapist for individual work.

Patients are often surprised to learn that they can enjoy a relationship that is not perfect. They also learn that the quality and depth of their relationships grow in direct proportion to what they are willing to invest. It is a moment worth celebrating when they announce their engagement to a suitable partner in the therapy session. It is clear then that a termination hour is soon to follow.

CHAPTER 8

The Patient's Relationship with the Therapist

Psychotherapy has evolved to help patients with many important psychological issues. Traditionally, effective therapy has helped patients to modify defenses that block out important feelings, to clarify misconceptions, to resolve unresolved relationship conflicts, to discover the source of feelings of inadequacy, to build self-esteem, and to widen the range of possibilities for coping with life. Psychotherapy has helped patients to restore a good balance between loving, working, and playing. There is another way in which psychotherapy helps impinged-upon adults. In addition to the working alliance and transferential relationship, impinged-upon adults must be allowed a real relationship with their therapist that encourages and guides the birth of a whole individuated self, separate from family.

BEGINNING THE THERAPEUTIC RELATIONSHIP

During the first hour with a new patient, therapists might ask themselves three critical questions basic to doing good psychotherapy for impinged-upon adults. If one or more of the answers is negative, another therapist may be better suited to conduct this psychotherapy. The first question is, Do I like this patient? If therapists do not like the patient, they will not be able to do the difficult work that lies ahead without reacting aggressively at a time when they need to clarify, confront, or interpret constructively. The second question is, Do I understand the central problem well enough to be able to treat this patient? If the central problem remains confusing, the patient should be referred to someone who can see it more clearly. The third question is important for all patients but is essential in the case of impinged-upon adults: Will I be able to separate from this patient when it is time for him or her to terminate? If therapists get too fond of, or dependent upon, a patient because of their own countertransference, they may provide a replica of what happened with the patient's parents instead of providing a healing, growth-producing environment where separation is the ultimate goal.

It may seem deceptively easy to form a relationship with impinged-upon adults during the initial phases of psychotherapy. This is sometimes referred to as the "honeymoon stage" or the stage of "transference cure." Patients are often extremely relieved to find a person who appears to understand and be supportive. Some patients respond with an immediate attachment that involves instant caring for the therapist. Most impinged-upon adults arrive on time and are eager to come for their hour. Overt resistance is minimal.

Most patients transfer a strong need to comply into the therapeutic setting and are skilled at intuiting exactly what they think the therapist is suggesting that they do. It is necessary to be wary of this phenomenon because patients may do something that is not in their best interest just because they perceive the therapist as suggesting or needing it. If the therapist appears troubled, this kind of patient will assume that they are responsible and will try to help.

In the early hours, patients may feel a need to prematurely resolve a presenting problem just to maintain the relationship with the therapist. Short-term therapy can sometimes successfully capitalize on this initial stage to help patients take a major step forward. During this time therapists may be misled about their effectiveness, feeling flattered or powerful. However, the patients' improvement precedes the full working alliance and real relationship necessary for growth. Both take longer to develop. The patients are more likely relating transferentially in the only way they know how.

In contrast to this overcompliance are patients who have learned to handle the pathological relationships within their families by being rebellious. In this case, the rebellion surfaces in the first hour and persists, presenting therapists with an entirely different kind of relationship.

Impinged-upon adults come into therapy with little trust unless they have had significantly healthy long-term relationships with persons outside the enmeshed family. Therefore, most patients must slowly build a sense of trust in the positive and supportive therapeutic alliance. At first, patients may feel as alone and unsure of this new kind of relationship as they would entering a different culture. They will feel mistrustful, while at the same time hoping that this new relationship will be helpful.

THE FIRST SENTENCE IN EACH HOUR

After a greeting in the waiting room, it is generally best to leave it to patients to begin the hour unless they are experiencing obvious difficulty. Therapists can suggest that the patients are the most qualified to open the hour because they best know their feelings, experiences, and events that have taken place since the last meeting. A patient's opening sentence is significant because it usually provides a reliable clue regarding the nature of the hour ahead. For instance, if the patient begins the hour with "I have thought about what we said last hour and have a lot more to tell you today," it is an indication that the patient is already at work without resistance or defense. On the other hand, if the patient begins the hour with a yawn and "I don't have anything particular to talk about today, and I can't remember the last hour," it signals a more defensive hour that requires a more active, confrontational stance from the therapist. Should the patient begin the hour with "I have something I've been meaning to tell you for a long time, but I haven't because I feel so embarrassed," the therapist may need to provide support for this difficult communication. When a patient sits down with an angry series of gestures or glares at the therapist silently, the therapist is called upon to help the patient figure out the disturbance in the therapeutic relationship by exploring how much the negative feelings are rightfully attributable to something inappropriate the therapist may have done and how much they may be transferred from a significant other in the patients' past.

THE THERAPISTS' USE OF THE COMMANDS

Much of the work with impinged-upon adults can be accomplished by listening carefully, not interfering when the patients are working well, refusing to rescue patients with a solution they can come to on their own, and confronting the patients' failure to proceed with the work (Masterson 1983). However, sometimes patients appear to run into a dead end. They either stop progressing or start to repeat information already given, for lack of knowing what else to say. This is where a knowledge of the commands is invaluable in terms of keeping the work moving forward. Such knowledge helps me to comment on, and to encourage patients with the work. If patients strongly confirm my statement and move forward with the work, I know that the information I have given them is accurate and that the patients are ready for this next step. However, discussing the commands directly with patients would rob them of the opportunity of discovering significant information themselves.

My use of the commands can also help me to take a statement made by patients and reframe or state it in a new form so that it can be seen from a different perspective. The following is a brief example.

Patient: I feel bad about not having had time to call my mother before I came here today. I feel as if I should ask you if I can use your telephone now.

Therapist: The word "bad" seems vague. Can you explain your feeling more?

Patient: It is not that *I* want to talk to *her*. It's that I feel worried.

Therapist: Worried for whom?

Patient: Not me, that's for sure! I must be worried that she is missing hearing from me. Oh yes, I'm worried that she will be mad at me for not doing the same thing each day at the same time. That's it! [maternal command 3]

Sometimes patients are unable to achieve this new outlook by themselves because the commands forbid it. The therapist, who is outside the enmeshed system, can encourage this new information.

Patient I: Mother spoiled me rotten and gave me everything I wanted.

Therapist: I think your mother gave you too much so you never learned how to experience the challenge of getting it yourself.

Patient II: It feels like no one in my family likes me.

Therapist: No one seems to be able to enjoy or support your steps forward.

Patient II: I don't care about anything for me anymore.

Therapist: I wonder if you mean you have strong feelings that you should fail obediently.

Patient IV: I feel like I was bad.

Therapist: I think you may not understand that the unnecessary criticism you have received is sabotage.

It is difficult to prescribe techniques for impinged-upon adults because any formalized interaction detracts from the *genuine* kind of relationship that these patients need. The commands serve as a general source of knowledge that therapists can draw on to understand their interaction from moment-to-moment with their patients.

THE LANGUAGE OF THERAPY

Many therapists are trained to avoid using any theoretical or technical language that will distance them from their patients. Instead, they speak in the language that patients introduce, facilitating the patients' ability to express personal feelings (Masterson 1976). This position generally seems valid, but a few terms can be helpful in bringing a new perspective to patients' experience. Two such terms are *impingement* and *entitlement*.

As patients try to express feelings more openly, it becomes evident that important concepts such as symbiosis and enmeshment are difficult for the patients to formulate themselves because the commands forbid such understanding. As patients attempt to clarify symbiotic enmeshment, it can be helpful to use the term *impingement*. Patients frequently confirm that this term expresses just what they are attempting to say. Their parents "impinged" upon them as children, and continue in adulthood to obliterate psychological and sometimes physical separation, without asking the patients. The patients thereby lose their "entitlement," or rights given at birth, to decide what to do and what to share or withhold.

THERAPISTS' STANCES WITH PATIENTS

Many therapists have received training in being a "blank screen" or a mirror for patients' feelings. This has traditionally called for therapists to hold back information about their own life so that patients could then freely project onto the therapists any transferred feelings from past relationships. Impinged-upon adults need to transfer feelings, but they also need the therapist to be more of a real person. Attempting to be a blank screen can be devastating for this kind of patient because it reminds them of the false self of their parents hiding the fragile real self. These patients feel as if they never really knew their parents, and they have a hard time if they feel similarly distanced from their therapist. The result is that the patients shut down.

Therefore, therapists need to be more spontaneous, real, and active without crossing the line into a social relationship or burdening patients unnecessarily with the therapists' own life situations (Angyal 1965, Greben 1984, Kaiser 1965, Lidz 1973, Masterson 1985, Taft 1962, Wells and Glickau 1986, and Winnicott 1965).

Such active therapists ought to be very versatile. Traditionally their work calls for

- silence when patients are working well.

- process comments, or comments and questions about what is happening with feelings and actions between patients and therapists.

- transference interpretations, or comments that clarify the feelings about past relationships that are brought forward into the therapeutic relationship.

- comments that encourage memories from the patients' past life experiences.

In addition, impinged-upon adults benefit from

- confrontation regarding unnecessary dependency.

- explicit support for growth.

- caring about patients as different and unique individuals.

- teaching, advising, and sharing information regarding a present problem. This may include selective sharing of the therapists' life experiences only if directly relevant to the problem under consideration.

- teasing patients as an alternative to confrontation.

- openly sharing and expressing with patients pain, sadness, and joy.

Therapists need to be whole, real persons. Then patients become able to try out a mature, intimate relationship.

If therapists had something negative happen in their own life which mildly intrudes on the therapy, the patients will detect it and may assume responsibility for the problem. Patients will avoid areas of concern to protect therapists. Therefore, it is appropriate for therapists to acknowledge the patients' sensitive, overprotective response and then address, directly but briefly, the issue that may be compromising the therapists' response to the patients. This response assures patients that the problem is the therapists' and clears the way for both of them to continue work.

Patients need a role model that is different from their

parents. They can benefit from seeing that the therapists have problems that can be handled with integrity, perseverance, and independence. Such demonstrations need to be concise and should be presented only when directly relevant to the patients' material.

The advent of a failed adoption required an abrupt change in my vacation schedule. Each patient was concisely informed about the loss of the infant and my changed working schedule. One patient, Margo, came to her next hour and watched me closely for a while.

Therapist: What are you thinking?

Margo (after a long pause, in which she seemed to weigh whether she could talk with me so personally): I have thought a lot about you and your life the last few days. You must be very sad. Are you all right? I really want to know. How can you go on working? Are you going to try to adopt again? Do you have the strength to start over again?

Therapist: Yes, I am going to try again. The pain my husband and I have felt tells us we would be missing too much if we gave up now.

Margo: Will my troubles seem small to you in comparison? (another pause) I thought about all the things I have lost too, for other reasons. We've both lost. And my losses are important too. If you can try again, and find another baby, then it stands to reason that I can quit bitching about my past and get on with what I want, too. You can have another baby and I can have a husband.

Therapists need to be flexible in another way. As has been noted, patients come into treatment with an incomplete psychological self. The development of a whole self tends to be uneven. Therapists must therefore be willing to move flexibly with patients from issues of basic trust to creativity to neurotic and oedipal issues until their incomplete self is filled in.

A therapist can actively support a patient's not taking on something that someone else wants him or her to do unless there is something in it for the patient. Patients are initially surprised by this stance and regard it as "the highest form of heresy." It is entirely out of their character but gradually they learn that it is a valuable guide. They realize that they are not just being "selfish" and that the best giving to others can occur when their own needs are also being considered and met.

It is possible to shorten the average treatment time by not always waiting for patients to talk about an issue that needs to be discussed. If patients present therapists with new material that indicates a new issue, the therapists can articulate that insight as soon as they understand it and feel that the patients are ready to hear it, instead of waiting for the patients to get to it on their own. It can be assumed that the patients are ready for a new step or the material would not have surfaced. If the patients are not ready to hear the issue, they can tell the therapists, who can then make a judgment as to whether to let it go or confront the unwillingness to proceed further. Patients seem to appreciate these insights that move the work along more quickly. Impinged-upon adults have already lost so much time, it seems undesirable to waste any more.

IMPINGED-UPON ADULTS' DECEPTIVE FRAGILITY

Many impinged-upon adults look fragile because they have been taught to do so and their lives have not been going well. Therapists may treat these patients as fragile, "going very slowly" and avoiding confrontation because the patients "aren't yet strong enough to handle it." Therapy can take years—with therapists acting like the patients' parents by treating them in a manner that prolongs psychotherapy.

It is a mistake to treat these patients as if they were fragile. Therapists may get into the position of feeling sorry for patients, thereby relieving the patients of their responsibilities within the therapeutic relationship. For instance, if patients undermine themselves in such a way that they lose a job, it may seem kind to let them postpone paying the bill for the psychotherapy. This is almost always a clinical error for several reasons. First, the therapists' leniency sends a not-so-subtle message that the patients can't really manage. Secondly, the therapists end up acting just like the patients' parents by picking up the tab. Resentment builds on both sides. The patients resent being viewed as incapable of paying, and the therapists resent late payment. Therefore, the working alliance is damaged. Therapists need to set limits, rather than encouraging or reinforcing failure in managing life, even if that means postponing the continuation of psychotherapy for a few sessions until the financial problem is worked out.

Experience shows that impinged-upon adults are not fragile; they have already survived a great deal of abuse. They can handle, and even appreciate, a confrontation that will enhance their own growth. Those patients who have assumed a passive-aggressive stance, using failure and rebellion as a way of punishing their parents, are in need of consistent, strong confrontation, some of the hardest work that therapists have to do. In contrast, those patients who have become overadaptive and compliant as a way of surviving need little confrontation, since this intervention only increases their overadaptivity. Compliant patients need to be encouraged to be less tuned in to others' needs, and more attentive to their own lives. They need to know that the primary goal is to get out of psychotherapy and on with living as soon as possible.

Masterson's view is that borderline patients should always be treated as if they could function in a normal manner (Masterson 1976, 1981, 1983). When and if they don't, the issue needs to be confronted until they fulfill their end of the contract. The therapists' expectation and respect for the patients' functioning becomes one of the most powerful tools in supporting the patients' growth. This is sometimes a difficult stance to maintain, because impinged-upon adults skillfully ask therapists to make things easier or to give the kind of gift that inhibits growth.

Therapists often fear that borderline patients have so many complex problems, it is useless to try to accomplish anything besides just listening, unless the patients can guarantee to spend a long time in therapy. However, my experience has shown that much can be accomplished with a knowledge of the unresolved issues and appropriate confrontation within a limited time, even if it is only three to six months. This may be necessary because some patients manage a growth step that moves them to another geographical location, putting a time limit on the therapeutic relationship.

RESPONSIBILITY

Patients frequently raise questions regarding the important issue of responsibility.

The following discussion has occurred many times with impinged-upon adults:

Arnold: How can you manage to see more than one or two patients during the same week?

Therapist: I am here to help, but the responsibility for the outcome of your life remains with each one of you.

Arnold (after a stunned silence): That is very interesting. This is going to be an issue between us, making the relationship difficult because my whole life has been spent taking responsibility for others.

Arnold and the therapist continued on to consider Arnold's additional assumptions and questions:

I have been expecting you to take care of me the way I took care of others.

Why haven't you solved my problems yet? Isn't that your job after all?

If you really take responsibility for me the way I took responsibility for my parents, won't you be too exhausted to see anyone else but me?

Therapists' clarity in presenting the issue of responsibility, both verbally and behaviorally, is critical for the successful treatment of impinged-upon adults (Kaiser 1965, Masterson 1983). Impinged-upon adults are accustomed to having their parents take unnecessary responsibility, in the form of rescuing the patients. In turn, deeply ingrained in patients is the need to take responsibility for the parents' defective sense of self. Therefore, it follows logically that impinged-upon adults expect therapists to take responsibility for their patients' lives.

This need for someone else to take responsibility is especially evident among patients who choose retaliation in response to poor parental caretaking. These adults keep returning home with a problem that worries their parents no matter how much it compromises their own growth and development. They convey to therapists their intention of trying to force their parents into finally taking the natural caretaking responsibility that would have been appropriate in the past. Unfortunately, the parents consort with this pattern of subversion.

Patients want therapists to fix a problem for them so that they do not have to risk working through painful feelings or to change their ways of relating to others. They not only expect it, but feel that they deserve it. Patients and therapists have to confront the difference between "rescuing" and "giving constructive help."

Therapists rescue when they do or say something that their patients could do for themselves. Therapists therefore need to decline invitations to rescue and should instead confront these manipulations. Therapists can effectively help only when patients have already done everything possible to advance the work and are taking responsibility for the quality of their own therapeutic work. This is the point at which therapists can provide some insight, explanation, or clarification.

Not taking unnecessary responsibility is a difficult task for therapists because the patients have modeled their parents' skill in asking to be rescued. If therapists truly decline invitations to help unnecessarily, impinged-upon adults go through a period of feeling angry, rejected, and unloved. If therapists fall into the trap of rescuing patients, as they do from time to time, the therapists are responsible for confronting this therapeutic failure so that the psychotherapeutic work can get back on course. The therapists' admission of error helps to further dispel the myth of perfection and usually launches patients back into the transferential working through.

However, therapists have to be careful not to overdo withholding help because patients may perceive this as sabotage. The issue of responsibility has to be combined with properly timed supportive discussion of new alternatives. Fortunately, declining to do something for patients that they can do for themselves automatically conveys one of the highest forms of respect and support. Therapists' clarity about the issue of responsibility helps patients with their confusion over this issue.

THE TWO PARTS OF PATIENTS

In a given psychotherapy hour, it is possible to see two different versions of the same patient. The first version usually presents itself in the first and second hours. This person is extremely perceptive and articulate about the problems at hand, has obvious capabilities, and is remarkably honest in expression of feelings. As soon as the psychotherapy gets more fully underway, the second version of this same patient emerges. This is the person the patient learned to be. This version of the patient works against therapists with such techniques as playing helpless, whining, complaining, being condescending or sarcastic, clinging, asking for more time, or manipulating for a rescue, and proclaims that failure is the only possibility. If therapists are not prepared for this version of the patient, they may feel let down and frustrated. This is the aspect of the patient that often baffles psychotherapists because such behavior appears to oppose therapeutic help. This second version has to be confronted and challenged. Once therapists have perceived it, it is not difficult to identify because there is usually a repetitive characteristic phrase or behavior that is a reliable clue that the failing version of the patient is in charge. As the psychotherapy proceeds, the patient will alternate between these two versions of the self, testing one against the other until one of them finally triumphs.

It is helpful to define these two differing aspects of the self for patients. The first is the capable part of the self. The second is the helpless or failure-prone part of the self created to survive within the family enmeshment. Initially, patients may feel embarrassed when therapists address these different versions, but gradually they learn to recognize when each part of the self is in operation, both during and outside of the hour. For example, with one patient, Rob, the therapist addressed the capable version of his self as "your own Rob" and the failure-prone version as "your parents' Rob." Patients can gain control over which self they present to the world.

PHYSICAL CONTACT BETWEEN PATIENTS AND THERAPISTS

Therapists are traditionally taught that any physical contact is inadvisable with patients (Langs 1973, 1974). Most patients have enough to handle just dealing with the verbal and emotional intimacy within the psychotherapeutic process. It is a comfort to patients to know that the therapist will not be physically intruding. However, there seem to be some exceptions in the case of impinged-upon adult patients. A therapist's hand on a patient's shoulder or elbow at the end of a difficult hour is a genuine way to provide support for the painful individuation process that is taking place. Bettelheim (1982) tells us that Freud shook hands with his patients at the beginning and ending of each hour.

On rare occasions patients may ask for a hug. It always appears to be a difficult request for them to make. Again the issue of entitlement is a strong one. They are not "supposed" to want it, and they must face their fear of engulfment. If they ask for it once as a way of expressing intimacy, as a way of accepting therapists' support, or as a way of saying good-bye at the end of the therapeutic relationship, it does not seem to disturb or retard the therapeutic relationship. On the other hand, the therapy becomes disrupted when hugs are repeatedly demanded out of clinging dependency, the need for reassurance, sexual need, or unresolved oedipal issues. Therapists must accurately intuit the difference often without much time to think about it.

PATIENTS' AWARENESS THAT THEIR FEELINGS ARE FELT BY OTHERS

Patients sometimes harbor the illusions that their therapist's relationship with them is the only relationship the therapist has. Therapists often have separate exit doors so that one patient does not have to run into the next patient. Therapists have been trained never to make references to other patients. However, it sometimes proves helpful to break this rule for impinged-upon adults. There are two reasons. First, they need to know that they have the same feelings as other impinged-upon adults because they have believed their feelings to be so out of place within their own families. Second, the illusion that their therapist has no other patients is a variety of the family myth of self-sufficiency. Impinged-upon adults need to have occasional reference to the fact that the therapist has a larger world than the therapist's relationship with them. That world is meaningful to the therapist, and in turn contributes to the therapist's relationship with them. This reality gives permission for patients to have their own larger world that does not include the therapist and enhances the therapeutic relationship.

SEPARATIONS FROM THE THERAPIST

With many kinds of psychotherapy, it seems wise to have a consistent pattern of regularly scheduled hours over an extended period of time. Impinged-upon adults are used to "closeness" without separations within their families. Therefore, separations that do come about because of vacations or therapists' occasional need to reschedule an hour may assume a temporary but necessary and important part of the total psychotherapeutic work. Therapists who take a national holiday but reschedule patients' hour into a later part of the week may be depriving patients of the opportunity to explore feelings about the separation. If the rescheduling is because therapists want a vacation but don't want to lose the income, they are behaving like the patients' parents, by considering only their own business needs and discounting the patients' valuable experience with separation.

Initially, separation evokes several predictable feelings from impinged-upon adults: feelings of being cut off, disapproval, and punishment. They fear that the therapist will forget about them completely and may never come back again. If patients have difficulty with object constancy, separation feels like the total loss of the therapeutic relationship. (The patients learned in childhood—command 11 from mothers—that separation meant death.) In adulthood, these feelings symbolize a psychological death because the patients' feeling of "being" has always come through being an extension of someone else. The patients may feel, at times, like a limb cut off from a body; the limb cannot feel pain, strength, or freedom to move without the blood supply from the rest of the body. As one patient said, "Not coming here is like being dropped off into a nothingness."

The following dialogue from a therapy hour illustrates both the feelings about separation and patients' relief after brief mention of the experience of other patients.

After a separation during the holidays, the patient, Leah, came to her appointment forty minutes early. She sat curled up in the corner of the waiting room couch looking unhappy. She started crying as soon as she sat down in the office.

Leah: I've had a horrible vacation, and I have been on the edge of tears all day. I'm so embarrassed that I can't get them to come out or go away.

Therapist: Well, now in the privacy of this office, perhaps you can let yourself cry and find out what you are feeling.

Leah explained that her mother reacted negatively toward her, first attacking and then rejecting her, because Leah had begun the painful process of becoming independent from her mother.

Therapist: Now go back to your tears and tell me how all this makes you feel.

Leah (sobbing): I feel alone . . . very small . . . betrayed, rejected, and as if I should probably kill myself.

Therapist (quietly): Why would you want to do that?

Leah: Life just doesn't feel worth living when I feel so alone and incapable. But it was just a feeling; I don't think about it seriously. When I drove away from my mother's house, I was crying so hard that I decided that it was dangerous to drive, so I pulled into a parking lot until I could calm myself. Then I drove very slowly and carefully the rest of the way home. There is no point in a car accident, because I might injure someone else. I just need to get used to being all by myself without running to my mother for the wrong kind of help.

Therapist: I am glad to hear that you are so sensible in taking care of yourself and other people. I wonder if part of your feeling of being alone and rejected is because of your separation from me during the holidays.

Leah (sobbing subsided): It must be because I felt so relieved when you came into the waiting room to get me. I needed to see that you are still here.

Leah and the therapist then worked on the dynamics between Leah and her mother and considered the degree of psychological pain that her mother must also be feeling.

Therapist: I think it's impossible for you to become a separate person in your own right without feeling this kind of pain. It is like the birth of a baby; it can't be done without labor. You seem to be feeling the way many of my patients do at this point in their separation from their parents. It is not unusual for you to feel momentarily suicidal as you have just reported. Your mother's response sounds pretty predictable too, in response to your changes. Remember that your mother doesn't consult with anyone about the changes that are going on the way you do. She sounds confused and scared.

Leah (relieved and more relaxed): My mother kept saying that I was crazy. I thought the way I was feeling, maybe she was right. Maybe it is more accurate to say that I just feel pain. I'm exhausted, sweaty, and sick to my stomach, but I'll be OK.

Patients cannot become whole, separate persons without going through feelings about separation. The experience comes during vacations in which the canceled hours are not rescheduled. During the initial separations, patients do not miss the therapist as much as they fear the separation. During these periods, patients visualize and practice their separateness and begin to feel it in a new way.

Tammy knew that her therapist frequently traveled out of town. She would visualize the car moving away from her until she could no longer see it. She feared that her therapist might have an accident and never return. During each successive trip, however, she became more comfortable as she increasingly realized that the therapist did return. The break in the therapeutic work was for a rest, not a reflection of her inadequacy. Even if the therapist did not think about her, Tammy could still exist as an independent and valuable person while they were apart. Gradually Tammy came to enjoy the separations as a time for her to be on her own. During a longer vacation, she was able to feel like a "satellite" in her "own orbit." She had enjoyed her time alone and came to the following hour both pleased to see the therapist and resentful that "the space ship was picking up the satellite again" when she was "just beginning to have a little bit of fun."

After a therapist's vacation, patients may come into the next psychotherapy hour confused about the differences between "missing," "needing," "clinging to," and "depending upon" the therapist. Sometimes patients will look sad or depressed but will say nothing about missing the therapist. Instead, they listlessly begin to cite failures, inadequacies, or worries that occurred while the therapist was on vacation. The therapist may well feel disconnected from the relationship during this monologue, while the patients are frustrated or angry about feeling "dependent" upon the therapeutic relationship. A closer look at the patients' activities during the therapist's absence may show that the patients actually coped well.

In fact, the patients missed the therapist but act as if they needed help and had failed. This is the only way they have been taught to express feelings after a separation. Frustrating feelings of dependency replace a natural sadness about separation. When this was pointed out to one patient, he said, "But I've always been led to believe that depression and sadness were bad feelings to have. How could you want to encourage those feelings from me now?" If patients can turn the feelings of dependency into appropriate sadness at the temporary loss of the therapeutic relationship, then they are on the way to healthily dealing with separations.

Patients' feelings about separations from the therapist change during the course of psychotherapy. Therapists have been trained to expect and elicit negative comments from patients about their reaction to a vacation. This training may be counterproductive during the latter part of the psychotherapy with impinged-upon adults if it forces therapists into interpreting something negatively that may not really be there. Impinged-upon adults reach a point when they anticipate a separation from therapists with positive feelings. They want it and enjoy it as a break from hard work. There is nothing unhappy to talk about; in fact, their pleasure about a vacation is something to celebrate. Any indication from therapists that a vacation should be upsetting is seen as parental dependency and sabotage. Therefore, it seems better for therapists to announce most vacations clearly and without questioning feelings, while simply watching to see how the patients react.

There are times when therapists must legitimately reschedule a regular appointment because their child is ill or there is a conference to attend or a lecture to give. If this happens infrequently and for a good reason, impinged-upon adults may appreciate the chance to help with the therapists' life problems or obligations by not coming in or by being willing to reschedule an hour. They appreciate it because they have rarely been able to aid their parents in a nonenmeshed way. Their parents tend to decline help because it makes them feel imperfect, and to see aid from their children as a disturbing statement of their children's mastery and independence.

THE THERAPIST'S RELATIONSHIP WITH THE PATIENT'S SPOUSE OR LONG-TERM MATE

In the medical model, it takes three persons to help someone with a physical problem: there must be a willing patient, a physician to do the medical procedure, and a nurse or caretaker to provide the steady psychological and physical before-and-after care. The treatment may deteriorate if any one of these three persons does not fulfill his or her responsibility. It is also helpful to have a triad in the psychotherapy process.

Ideally, there is a willing patient, a psychotherapist, and a third party to handle the support role. This third party is frequently a spouse, a mate, or a good friend, with whom patients have a healthy relationship. Patients may not have someone initially, but the process of psychotherapy will help such a relationship to evolve. Patients need someone to "be" with when there is psychological pain, between psychotherapy hours. This person listens nonjudgmentally, is able to leave patients alone when they are in a bad mood, and confronts patients when they are behaving inappropriately.

These significant others are in an inherently difficult position because therapists are an invisible third party in the relationship between patients and their significant others. The patients bring feelings to their therapists previously shared only with their significant other or not shared at all. The therapists will be talking about the significant other and making changes that will affect that person. The significant others may need to have some information about what is going on in the psychotherapy. Sometimes, it becomes advisable for therapists to meet patients' significant other at least once, of course with the patients' consent. It may be a brief contact in the waiting room, or third parties may join a psychotherapy session. The latter may be beneficial for at least two reasons: significant others get a chance to see who the therapist is, to ask questions, and to develop their own perspective on what is going on; this helps to establish trust that the process will ultimately result in constructive changes both within the patients and within the relationships between the patients and the significant others. Again, it may provide understanding about the underlying issues and how best to respond to the patients in difficult circumstances.

Significant others should be kept in mind as the psychotherapy progresses because these third parties can be deeply affected. From time to time, therapists may want to send messages to third parties that consider their feelings, clarify what is going on, and respect their rights in the relationship. This temporarily offers support to third parties in staying within the helping role and seeing the psychotherapy through to its end. Patients carry these messages voluntarily and do not seem to regard them as any violation of confidentiality.

This policy is much debated among psychotherapists because it involves a sharing of a relationship that is designed to be private. However, the advantages generally outweigh the disadvantages. Significant others are able to ask appropriate questions, give patients and therapists valuable information, and be very supportive of patients' work. Patients are often proud to briefly share aspects of the psychotherapy relationship with their significant other and their loved-one. Meetings with these third parties will be few, and can be requested by any one of the three concerned parties, but only for a reason that promotes forward progress. The basic privacy of the therapeutic relationship is maintained.

Significant others who do not meet the therapist are in an inherently difficult position because they must change with the patients, but without any help because they have no one to consult. They may be afraid the patients will discover through psychotherapy a desire to leave the relationship with the significant other. If it is a solid relationship created for healthy reasons rather than unresolved dependencies, it will likely survive and deepen.

What happens to present relationships that are enmeshed or based upon past unresolved conflicts? These are the relationships in which the third parties may try to undermine the psychotherapy rather than to help. As patients understand and resolve their conflicts, there is sometimes a need to confront, modify, or leave the relationship if their partner is unable to make constructive changes with the patients. These are the relationships that give psychotherapy the unfortunate reputation of "breaking people apart."

Similar support can be offered to patients' parents. Unfortunately, most of the time, they choose to go without it. Their level of deception does not allow them to consider the enormity of the pathological enmeshment for which they need help.

LENGTH OF TREATMENT

Knowledge of the commands and experience gained through case material make it possible for therapists to shorten psychotherapy. Impinged-upon adults can often afford to come only once a week. Together they and their therapist can do a satisfactory job involving a deep understanding of the problem and a working through of the feelings in a period of from 50 to 150 hours (1 to 3 years), the average being somewhere around 120 hours (2 years). This amount of time makes patients feel that they are taking on a reasonable financial and emotional investment that might well achieve a desired goal.

Sometimes patients come to therapists with an externally imposed time limit that only allows for a very short contract of 10 to 20 sessions. Even in that limited time period, it is still possible to meaningfully address the overall issue of enmeshment in a

ows patients to see themselves and their relation-
ers differently (Davanloo 1978, Mann 1973, Small
rg 1980).

DIFFICULT ASPECTS OF TREATMENT

Even with understanding, there are several aspects of the psychotherapy that seem exhausting in treating impinged-upon
adults. One is these patients' pervasive underlying drive against
the psychotherapy growth process and toward failure and regression as the main means of preserving a relationship. A
second is therapists' feeling that patients may summarily dismiss
the therapists if the patients are displeased with them, much as
the patients' parents threatened to abandon the patients. A third
difficult aspect is surviving and cutting through patients' defenses that have been created to fend off their parents but also
work to hold back the therapeutic relationship.

To survive these constant threats, therapists must understand the process fully enough so that their feelings are not
continually hurt or frustrated. Therapists must instead hold a
steady and consistent course that allows for forward progress
without hesitation or undue discouragement.

THE TERMINATION, OR GRADUATION, PROCESS

I used to think that a good psychotherapy resulted in one final
termination. If patients needed to return or contact their therapist, it meant that the previous work was deficient in some way.
If patients had to leave before the work was fully completed
because of external life circumstances, that meant that the patients were resisting. In contrast, it is possible to adopt a much
more flexible attitude toward the termination process. It is,
perhaps, better viewed as a graduation. There are many different graduations incorporated in the educational process, with
resting periods in between these steps. The same should be true
of psychotherapy. Therapists should be available to their pa-

tients, much as their family physicians, to help with a particular problem when, and if, it arises.

Patients appear to know best when it is time to stop. This usually occurs when the presenting problem or symptoms have diminished to the patients' satisfaction (Gardner 1985). It is possible for therapists to anticipate patients' initial request to consider a graduation simply by noting the therapist's enjoyment regarding the obvious growth that has taken place.

Psychotherapy does not take the difficulty out of life. Instead it enriches and expands people's horizons, perhaps leading them beyond into greater complexity. People will always be confronted with problems. Patients leave when they are ready to take on life alone. Many patients will do a sizable piece of work to solve one problem, go off alone, and return several years later for additional help with a new challenge. They return because the previous therapy was useful. Some patients need to leave prematurely as a way of working through the separation issues (as described in the vignette that follows). If this is the case, they will return to finish the work.

Exceptions to this rule are patients who may want to "abort" because the pain is too great. I try to halt this kind of termination with consistent support and understanding regarding the pain. Occasionally, patients will leave because they want to hold on to their pathology and they realize that I will not accept that. Sometimes patients leave the therapeutic relationship to test the therapists' ability to allow separation.

Margaret was faced with the issue of a premature termination in the middle of her work because her husband's insurance terminated when he moved to a new job. This crisis allowed her to transfer onto me everything that she had been taught by her parents about leaving relationships. In the five hours remaining, she raised the following critical issues, demonstrating her awareness of seven of the commands. My responses demonstrate the use of some of the permissions.

First, because of her transferential feelings, she was terrified to tell me that she wished to stop therapy. She was convinced that I would react as her mother did: I would become angry with her (maternal command 7); I would feel that Margaret was rejecting me because I was not competent (maternal command 3); I would tell Margaret that she hadn't tried hard enough to get additional funds, and that she was allowing her husband to run her life while forgetting the importance of the patient–therapist relationship (maternal command 2). If that tactic failed, I might convince her to stay by saying that she was not well enough to leave (maternal command 5).

Margaret and I worked together with these transferred feelings.

Therapist: I support your wish to stop therapy when the insurance no longer covers it, especially if you thought you were coming to see me to support *my* self-esteem [maternal permission 1]! Is there any other reason *you* have been coming to see me? Have you accomplished what *you* want [maternal permission 3]?

Margaret: I really have had no clear agenda for myself. I stole moments of the hour for me [maternal command 1]. [crying] I have never thought about leaving [maternal command 3].

She discovered that the issue of her departure was up to her and that I would let her leave. She then displaced her feelings of sadness about leaving me onto absent family members.

Margaret: I have nothing for us to talk about today [maternal command 8]. Because I am going to leave, I expect you to be petulant and uninterested anyway, so why should I bother. I know that there is more work to do, but I have already managed to bury those issues, so they are now forgotten.

As long as the insurance paid for a large portion of each hour, Margaret didn't really have to deal with the issue of whose hour this was.

Margaret: Is this hour yours because you are supposed to cure me, or is it my husband's because he sent me to deal with my bad behavior?

Therapist: If it is indeed your hour, have you finished [maternal permission 6]? Perhaps you want to leave to find out how I will react [maternal permission 8].

Margaret: What would happen if I stopped for a while and then called you again? [She hypothesized the rejection that she was accustomed to from her family.] I'll bet you'd be angry. You will retaliate by saying that you don't have time to see me or that I must come in at a time inconvenient for me. Or you might only give me part of your attention [maternal command 7]. Perhaps you will manipulate me to come back by rescuing me with a gift of a very low fee [maternal command 4].

Therapist: I only want you to do what you want to do [maternal permission 9].

Margaret: I still do not know what I think about relinquishing this hour. It would feel like a gift if I could come back because I have gotten so much out of the work we have done together. I fear that the only way I could return would be to arrange a crisis. Then my husband would send me back and you would have to take me in [maternal command 5]. Or, maybe a a gift of money would drop out of the sky [magical thinking].

Therefore, when she wants something for herself, the only two ways she can get it are to fail or to hope for magic. She cannot be assertive.

She could not tell her husband how much the psychotherapy had meant to her because she feared he would feel threatened that she had felt intimacy with me [maternal command 2]. She was surprised to consider that her husband might appreciate and benefit from the intimacy that she had allowed herself with me [maternal permission 9].

Therapist: You are entitled to evaluate our relationship in terms of what it means to you—both its negative and positive aspects [maternal permission 7]. You have never thought to do this. It has not occurred to you to consult with me or your husband about your psychotherapy because you assumed we would control you.

She was learning through her exploration of this issue that intimacy includes letting a person come and go as they have the need (maternal permission 3).

By the end of the final hour she had decided to leave with the considerable gains that she had made. It seemed that she left because she had to test, rather than talk about, my response to her needs to separate both physically and psychologically. Most important, she had made the decision by herself and for herself. She promised herself to return when she felt ready. Six months later, she sent a card expressing appreciation for my help and suggesting that she would be calling me again soon. Then she returned to finish her work.

Therapeutically, the graduation phase can be difficult to manage. It takes time because the patients have never really experienced an acceptable "good-bye" with a significant other. Patients find it hard to believe that leave-taking would be sanctioned and supported by the therapist.

Patients may be in a hurry to leave as soon as they acquire a sense of separate self and can freely disobey the family commands. They want independence and are acutely aware of what they have lost. At this point impinged-upon adults can leave home psychologically, as well as physically, and are able to express ideas and affection with greater freedom and trust that others will honor their needs.

Before their departure, it is optimal for patients to practice this newly found trust and affection with the therapist. They now feel lovable, have love to give to others, and feel indebted to the therapist for providing the therapeutic relationship.

However, natural affection and the ability to love, practiced within the therapeutic relationship, must then be withdrawn and turned to others who are able to return it more fully than therapists within the structured fifty-minute working hour of psychotherapy. The relationship has served its purpose by ultimately freeing patients to invest their love more fully elsewhere. This realization presents patients with another painful moment. They may be impatient about wanting to "make up for lost time" and to put their affection in a place where it can be more fully reciprocated. It is difficult for therapists to balance supporting the graduation process of a newly individuated self and, at the same time, suggesting a proper and affectionate good-bye.

If patients leave too early, the pain of loss will continue longer. The therapist has been of help with only a few hundred hours of support for growth. It is hard-won and financially expensive support that patients were entitled to have earlier in life without charge.

Most patients have parents still living, some close by. The patients need to continue to deal with them in a reasonable manner that preserves the relationship but is minimally importuning to themselves. The irony for patients is that they must leave the nurturing relationship with the therapist and continue with the psychopathological one with the parents.

Some patients choose to keep in contact on occasion with a card, a call, or stopping by the office to share news of their next achievement. These contacts are infrequent and generally mean that the patients are touching base again with an important person.

There is pain for the therapists too. This job requires psychotherapists who are willing to grow and able to handle and support multiple separations. Impinged-upon adults enter the office for the first time confused by the fact that life has gone wrong. The therapists must watch, listen, and intervene to recapture each patient's potential. Patients begin to handle life with an understanding they didn't have before, accomplish what they need to do and leave, just as they should. Many, in the process, become people that would make good friends, had they and the therapists met under different circumstances. They leave, and the therapists may grieve the loss.

Patients make a long journey by the time they are ready for graduation. They have pulled away from a family environment believed to be perfect, warm, and close. They understand the destructive nature of that relationship to growth. They have given up the temptation to be taken care of in a regressive way and have refused the offer of an allegedly "easy life" if they serve their parents. They are alone and separate, finding out that life is as difficult for them as it is for other people.

Alice expressed her feelings about graduation by saying, "I think I can get ready to go now because I know that I am not a part of my mother. Instead, it is now only my mother still trying to be a part of me."

During the graduation process, one patient summed up what her psychotherapy had meant to her. She had only worked with me for one year because of a professional opportunity that she had accepted across the country. Before she left she said, "What my mother taught me is that I need to fail, to get attention. I construed that as love. What I've learned here is that I have to do the very best I can with my life. That will be quite sufficient and people will respond, more than likely, with love and caring."

Ben said in his graduation hour, "I used to feel inadequate and less than anyone else because of my problem background and consequent difficulties. I don't feel that way any more. In fact, if anything, I feel stronger than the average person because I have looked at my own personal horror. I know what it is like to be on both sides of the fence now, and I feel the wiser for it. I am like a person who has received a small-pox shot: I have some of the pox in me and it will always be there, but I also have the antibodies. I will be able to share what I have learned with others, especially my children. I have been successful with you and I feel good."

The unconscious mind gives patients and therapists information that the patients are ready for graduation. The patients' dreams are generally clear and therefore easy for the patients to interpret. One patient reported the following two dreams with his own interpretation during his next-to-last therapy hour.

I dreamt that I was in a forest camping out, and two characters came along that were obviously up to no good. Suddenly I became Paul Bunyan and went over and picked one up in each of my huge hands. I restrained them from doing any harm. The two men were my parents, and now I know that I am in control of what they can do with me. I didn't kill them.

My fiancée and I went down into a subway and looked at the map only to discover that this subway was just a spur and only went to a dead end. We turned around and got our money back and left. This dream reminds me that I can tell when a relationship is not good for me and I have the capability to get out of it.

CONCLUSION

As my experience doing psychotherapy has increased, I have found myself moving more and more in the direction of providing a relationship for patients that is relatively open, as human as possible, and explicit in its caring and honesty. Sometimes I have to fight a feeling of guilt that I am bending, if not breaking, some of the traditional rules of therapy.

As I have wrestled with these issues, I have wondered if some of our language and our manner with patients is more to protect our need as therapists for omnipotence and distance from intimacy than it is to provide an uncontaminated and optimal environment for patients' feelings. My patients wonder with me why we call people "objects" and talk about "termination" rather than "graduation" or "celebration." As one patient said, "The word *termination* implies that you never want to see me again!" Why do we use such cumbersome phrases as "libidinal unavailability" and write about people in a style of jargon that makes them sound like something less than human? Feelings are best expressed in an atmosphere of openness and caring. To provide this, therapists must be willing to risk ethical intimacy with every patient contact.

CHAPTER 9

Therapeutic Issues and the Therapeutic Process

Patients and therapists discuss many issues over the course of therapy. They consider present relationships and problems, the presence of commands or myths, past memories of significant others, and the relationship occurring between them. The following therapeutic issues, questions, and processes seem to appear consistently in the psychotherapy of impinged-upon adults.

DEFINING THE DIFFERENCE BETWEEN FAILURE AND IMPINGEMENT

When patients want to take a step forward but hesitate, the question that should be asked is *why*. The consistent response is, "I am afraid that I am going to fail." Conceptually, patients are afraid to succeed and at the same time experience fear of failure. This feeling is accurate because the myth of self-righteous perfection dictates that they never did anything quite right. The lack of positive recognition from their parents for growth steps means failure to patients. Impinged-upon adults experience a lack of success when they have actually done well.

Impinged-upon adults tend to view their lives in terms of degree of failure. They have not gotten where they wanted to go;

it does not occur to them to look at the situation as anything other than their fault. They do not see themselves as potentially successful people who have tried to keep moving ahead. Therapists can help them to define the difference between failure and impingement with the following analogy.

A runner runs a race. If he did not bother to practice and cannot make it around the track in good time, one could say he failed. However, if he practices a lot and runs as fast as he can but loses the race because someone mistakenly puts several wooden hurdles in his lane only, it is reasonable to use the word *impingement*. He has been impinged upon by an external source; it is not his own inability or lack of motivation to perform. He must clear the obstacles away. Even if impinged-upon adults manage to scale the barriers, they feel as if they failed because the accomplishment causes so much psychological distress.

Nancy said, "I am a failure in getting to psychotherapy on time." In reality, before I could see her, she had patiently waited several weeks without losing her motivation. She managed to get the necessary referral for insurance purposes from an unsympathetic physician. Then on her way to my office she circumvented traffic that had ground to a halt because of an accident. Despite these obstacles, she arrived at her session only ten minutes late and did some good work. I pointed out that Nancy had been successful in getting around several obstacles, but she seemed to feel like a failure merely because the obstacles were there.

Tim came to the psychotherapy hour feeling triumphant because he had been able to find a way around several "snags" in his graduate school electronics assignment. He explained that he had erroneously learned from his parents that a problem is a "signal to stop working." He had never been told that problems are a normal part of the challenge of living, merely something to surmount. He lived in "dread of snags" because they seemed like unfair obstacles outside of his control.

THE FIGHT FOR SUPREMACY BETWEEN THE SABOTAGING SELF AND THE SUCCEEDING SELF

Success in life makes impinged-upon adults anxious and therefore only marginally happy. First, they are afraid of abandonment. Then they are surprised at how much hard work living is, and miss being "rescued" by their parents. As patients progress, periodically there are some therapy hours in which it is obvious that they are doing extremely well while trying hard to convince the therapist of their failure. The patients keep regression in the picture to protect their relationship with their parents and, transferentially, with their therapist.

Patients get angry with their therapist for not buying into the sabotaging self and frustrated when the therapist does not rescue them from their hard work by giving special help.

Andrea was attending a course that provided important preparation for an entrance examination. During the first class meeting her sabotaging self reigned completely. She worked slowly, answered sample questions incorrectly, and came home feeling "like a dummy." After her hour of psychotherapy, she went back to the second class. She had stomach pain all the way to the class and feared that she might vomit. She went into the ladies' room and looked at her reflection in the mirror. She said, "You will take this class no matter how many times you have to throw up. You will sit near that door so you can leave to vomit if you have to. You will come back into class." Her nausea went away, and she started to work. She did well for the remainder of the course and achieved a high score on the entrance examination.

This is an excellent example of a patient's ability to let the succeeding part of her self triumph over the self-defeating part. She was proud of her understanding and her ability to do something constructive about it.

ENTITLEMENT AND HAPPINESS VERSUS THE FEAR OF DEATH

The feeling that one is *entitled* to reasonable help goes hand-in-hand with a positive and supportive relationship. Impinged-upon adults have little sense of the meaning of reasonable help. They are more skilled at failing for the purpose of eliciting unnecessary help and "taking care" of the therapist than they are at taking care of themselves. For example, they tend to clock-watch for therapists, making sure that they get only their allotted time. They are anxious if therapists choose to extend the hour by a few minutes. They do not believe that if they want something reasonable, they can simply ask for it because the person they ask might be uncomfortable saying no.

The issue of *entitlement* comes up in relation to telephone calls to therapists between hours. Although some discomfort is a normal part of psychotherapy, there are times when a legitimate need arises for telephone contact with therapists. During the initial stages of therapy, many patients are unable to act on this need, even if therapists offer their availability when the situation warrants. In the next hour, their therapist may hear about painful meetings with their family or sleepless nights of working through alone. A five-minute phone contact might have helped. Sometimes therapists can encourage them to take advantage of this phone privilege by saying, "I would rather talk with you for just a few minutes in a way that would be helpful than to hear later that you had such a long, sleepless night." Such patients spend hours wondering whether or not they have the right to make the call.

It is only fair to say that the issue of telephone calls tends to be complex for this kind of patient anyway. The pathologically symbiotic part of impinged-upon adults wants therapists to magically intuit when they are upset and call them, as the impinged-upon adults have to do with their parents. A vast majority of enmeshing parents have manipulated their children into calling daily or at least several times a week. Patients often report an expense of up to hundreds of dollars a month for calls to their families. They are expected to call their parents, while their parents rarely call them. If patients do not call, there is silence from their parents for a time, and then an irate or tearful guilt-provoking telephone call to say "How could you do this to me?" The patients are resentful of being required to telephone, especially when they come to understand just how much these contacts are solely for maintaining their parents.

Opposing the feeling of entitlement is a fear of death. Most patients are better acquainted with this fear than any sense of entitlement. In fact, they fear and expect death daily, especially when they have just completed a new step forward. This fear is the result of having been repeatedly threatened with abandonment. When the patients were children, abandonment meant death (Masterson 1976). The fear of dying is the logical consequence of stepping away from taking care of their parent in adulthood.

Arleen finished writing a book with a co-author with whom she had been enmeshed. It was due to be published shortly. She said, "My co-author would like it if I fell off a cliff now that I have finished the hard work so that she can have the glory." During that week, she feared death by a car accident but did not connect her fear with her statement about her co-author.

Jackie worked the hardest she had ever worked to find a job for herself. During that same week she had a dream in which someone came up to her and said, "Now you are going to die." She was led into another room and directed to die. She did, but discovered that she felt no different after she had died. The dream reassured her that the threat of death was not real.

Many patients fear death by a serious illness, especially cancer. A scratch that runs into a mole becomes a major concern about a cancerous melanoma. These patients need to be able to talk about the various ways in which they fear death; they need advice as to whether they really need to act on their fear by consulting a physician. Such patients tend to live life fiercely because they expect it to be snuffed out at any moment. To die is the logical extension of the fear of being "caught," "left," "hated," and "rejected." It is a difficult way to live. Therapists' reassurance and interpretations can be tremendously helpful.

There is an additional reason for patients to raise the issue of death. Some patients temporarily consider taking their own lives. Most will be quick to acknowledge that they are not truly suicidal in the sense of feeling the deep despair that makes one want to bring an end to one's life. Instead, they think about death because the truth revealed in their psychotherapy is painful and suicide is the only way they can think of to make it go away. They consider death as a substitute for the pain of psychological incompleteness and abandonment by their parents (intrapsychic or real). In addition, the issue of death may come up because they want to go back to the most basic entitlement: deciding for themselves whether or not to live. Then they must decide if they will live for themselves or exist only as extensions of others.

Along with the fear of death comes avoidance of pleasure. Happiness is hard-won, and when it first comes it feels frightening. Many patients say quietly "I feel happy" while fear crosses their faces. If something good happens, patients are likely to be very quiet and offhanded about it. In fact, it is the absence of joy that is one of the hallmarks of the lives of impinged-upon adults. As one patient's mother said, "The good times are just a respite from the bad times."

Impinged-upon adults need time to realize that they have not been happy. They tend to confuse happiness with being special to their parents and are led to believe that being special "feels good." But to be special to their parents, they have to avoid loving others and mastering life experiences, richer sources of true happiness. There comes a point in the psychotherapy when patients have to choose between symbiotic specialness and being happy as an independent, productive person. In the process of sorting this out, patients may attempt to become a therapist's special patient. There is a sharp distinction between a therapist's liking the independent person that a patient is becoming and feeling that a particular patient is "special." Patients are surprised when told that they are in trouble if they become their therapist's special patient because that probably means that the therapist needs them to fill some incomplete part of himself or herself.

PATIENTS' DIFFICULTY WITH TAKING VACATIONS

It is difficult for impinged-upon adults to spend money on a vacation to get away from everything to relax and be happy without a lot of attendant anxiety.

Alan came to his psychotherapy hour just before leaving for a vacation with a friend. He claimed to have "nothing to talk about today" and recognized that he felt "shut down." Even though he had carefully scheduled his time away so that he would not miss a therapy hour, we figured out that he was anxious that I would disapprove of his plans to relax. If he was already "shut down," he felt that he could better protect himself from my abandoning of him. Part of him wanted me to object to his vacation and request that he stay home because such an action on my part would make him feel important to me. In addition, he recognized that he felt guilty about not being at home for his parents' weekly phone call and was afraid of the intimate thoughts that he had about the girlfriend going with him. Finally, two neighbors had offered to take care of his bird. He was afraid of rejecting one neighbor's offer. These thoughts culminated in a nightmare about not getting to the train station on time and being prevented from getting on the train by the conductor. He awoke arguing vehemently with the train conductor. He could catch only glimpses of fantasies of relaxing and being happy on the upcoming vacation.

Once we had analyzed the dream, Alan was pleased to discover his emerging ability to fight back with the conductor (his parents) for some time to relax and to be happy.

THE FIGHT BETWEEN THE FALSE AND REAL SELVES

Ann talked about her fight between her false self and her real self by saying, "I submerged myself so deeply to cope with my parents that I don't know who I am inside."

As has previously been pointed out, impinged-upon adults have developed a false self that carefully watches and attends to the needs and commands of others for the purpose of avoiding abandonment. This false self operates automatically, hiding what there is of the real person underneath, and is a frustrating obstacle to what patients otherwise should be feeling (Balint 1968, Masterson 1983, Winnicott 1958, 1965).

In addition, the false self often demonstrates proficiency, appears self-sufficient, and provides little interaction with the therapist. When the false self reigns, patients usually feel safe and protected during the hour but realize soon after leaving that none of their questions were answered and little contact was made. This ability of the false self to hide real concerns can make a session very frustrating for both patients and therapists.

Patients also have to fight the myth of self-righteous perfection (see Chapter 4) along with the false self. Impinged-upon adults believe that they must "do it right" to be able to maintain the therapeutic relationship. This self-imposed demand obscures the patients' own feelings. It is especially frustrating for patients when therapists do not tell them what they (the therapists) "need." As the patients try to guess, anxiety mounts, with an ensuing loss of a sense of themselves. The therapeutic relationship, which the patients value, then comes to a standstill.

Sometimes patients try to protect themselves from this frustrating circumstance by pretending that they do not value the therapeutic relationship. Then they can thus feel somewhat more relaxed, which allows the relationship to progress more easily. The issue of entitlement is at the core of this problem, too, because the patients feel that their affection for their therapist can only be expressed by meeting the therapist's needs. At this point, the therapist can help by reflecting the process just described. This is often successful, enhancing the patients' understanding and allowing them to regain a sense of their real self.

The false self implies something negative to be gotten rid of, while the real self is good, to be fully exposed. Sometimes patients strive to come up with the real self in an overadaptive, false-self way.

It seems more productive for patients to think of the false self as having had a critical adaptive and protective function in the past. It is a valuable part of the self, to be retained in numerous work and social situations. The false self of some patients is impressive, allowing them to be proficient at teaching a class or handling an administrative assignment. If the false self is not rejected by therapists as simply a defense, the real self can begin to emerge from behind it.

As patients begin to differentiate between the false self and the real self, they encounter many frustrating moments of trying to make the shift from one to the other. The false self tends to serve a protective function within the therapy. It reasserts itself after a vacation or other interruptions in therapy, a confrontation or an argument with the therapist, a major insight, or an important step forward. Recognizing and respecting its presence as a protection can often lead to a profitable discussion about what needs to be protected. As the therapy proceeds, there tends to be less false self, more real self, and a progressive integration of these two parts of an emerging whole person.

Actually, patients often know their own feelings, but they

become confused because they have been taught by a symbiotic family that it is only possible to have "one feeling at a time." That feeling is supposed to be positive toward the family. Therefore, feeling both happy to see family again and sad because of the obvious limitations in interaction makes patients feel "crazy," disloyal, and bad.

OBJECT CONSTANCY

Patients develop positive feelings of affection and trust for therapists, causing a low-level anxiety for the patients. Basic to entitlement and a supportive relationship is the issue of object constancy, whether or not patients have a visual memory or picture of their therapist when not in the therapist's presence. If patients feel like mere extensions of other people, they tend not to focus in on and recognize other persons as separate wholes. Therefore, some patients cannot visualize their therapist in between hours. When patients are asked about this, they frequently say something like "I don't have a picture of you, but I do have a sense of your presence." That "sense" may be something like a feeling for the colors in the therapist's office. One patient said, "When I try to call on a picture of you in my head, I come up with a huge picture of my father instead. I am beginning to get a picture of you, but you are very small compared to him, and very vague. I really have to work on what you look like and push him aside." This comment suggests that this patient feels conditioned by her parents not to truly notice anyone outside the family.

Patients who have achieved some degree of object constancy within other relationships occasionally and temporarily lose this ability in their relationship with their therapist. Since this developmental skill has been achieved in other relationships, it may be that the lack of complete object constancy within the therapeutic relationship is an issue of entitlement rather than a developmental failure.

At first, Jessica realized with surprise that she could not clearly remember what I looked like. Next, she acquired a black-and-white inner image of my head, excluding my eyes and mouth. Then she reported an image of a stern-looking mug shot in a black turtleneck. She saw me as a convict, a reflection of her ambivalence about whether I was a person to be trusted or an enemy of her as yet much-needed family enmeshment. Next she reported a full color picture of me but only from the back. One day she was surprised by a very clear picture of me which stayed with her for about a day. She did not have the control to make it go away. Finally, she acquired a full front view of me in color. She was able to maintain this picture, unless there was a vacation or a disturbance in the therapeutic relationship. Over time, she acquired full control of the object constancy.

A person who has gained or regained object constancy feels an inner sense of companionship and calm. As one patient said, "I am not alone in here (pointing to heart area) anymore now that I can see you anytime I want in my head."

Another effect of impinged-upon adults' lack of object constancy is that they do not expect therapists to remember the details of their psychotherapy in between sessions. Many patients will automatically offer to fill therapists in on details already explained or will pause to ask, "Do you remember?" It is very important for therapists to keep a written record of each psychotherapy hour to review before the next therapy session so that they can remember those relevant names and details accurately.

There are some ways in which patients can facilitate the acquisition of object constancy. They have figured out ways to acquire a few simple items that can be used as transitional objects between psychotherapy hours. A common one is a tissue used during the hour (Winnicott 1958, 1965). Instead of throwing it away, they take it with them. Sometimes that one tissue can be carried for a long time in a pocket or in the car. It is simply a reminder that the office, the hour, and the therapist are still there. Other patients help themselves to a business card, sometimes taking away one each hour. One patient reported tacking them up on her bulletin board, which gave her a concrete record of her growing commitment to the relationship. One therapist, when requested to by patients, would write the most important message from the hour in a single sentence on a piece of paper and give it to them. Another patient asked for a small picture of his therapist to help maintain a visual awareness of the therapist outside of the hour. His request made the therapist think that perhaps more impinged-upon adults might benefit from a small professional photograph of their therapist on a business card. Finally, therapists can directly encourage their patients to look at them carefully, giving their patients permission to concentrate and visually memorize the therapists' physical appearance.

THE PROCESS OF GAINING SEPARATENESS

Patients' parents have offered them a false sense of security in a pathological way by advising the patients to stay away from "change." Patients therefore tend to define change as "giving up something" instead of "adding something new."

One patient, Nancy, evinced especially severe pain over her separation from her family in her initial evaluation.

Nancy had decided to move across country to take a new, high-paying job. She was able to say good-bye to her family and friends and to pack her belongings. However, when she arrived, she began to feel an anxiety that reached panic proportions. It kept her up at night, unable to sleep or even lie down, and made her unable to take any steps to find new living quarters. She felt a tremendous restlessness, mitigated only mildly by a constant pacing, an "out of control" feeling as though she were having a "nervous breakdown." The only thing that calmed her briefly was a phone call to her parents. We discussed the separation issues likely making her anxious, but it was impossible for her to consider a psychotherapy with me because my office was so far from her home. First she had to reduce her anxiety. She decided to return home immediately and seek psychological help where she was more comfortable.

Another patient tackled the same problem from a different vantage point.

Michele spent some time talking about an unusual scene in the middle of New York City. While walking down the street, she saw a young man join a painting crew working on a new building. He picked up an empty paint can and a clean paint brush. He began "to paint" the trim of a window with the same expert motion as the other painters.

Quite a crowd had collected to watch his performance with invisible paint. Michele watched for a long time, amused and envious of how easily this "fake" painter violated the expectations of everyone around him. He did exactly what he wanted. Michele recognized that this man might be a little crazy. But she recognized something she could not do herself: she was unable to "fool" people; instead, she could only conform to their expectations.

During the period of gaining separateness, patients usually have many dreams expressing their feelings of fear, doubt, guilt, and impending punishment. These dreams reflect the sudden and irrational sabotaging turns that parents have taken to prevent their children from separating.

One patient, Janet, reported the following dream after a step forward in her professional life.

Three policemen came to my house because two numbers on my credit card were reversed. In addition, I was about to be accused of a crime I didn't commit. There was no way to present my point of view.

Janet realized that the three policemen were her parents and the one sister who was still symbiotically attached to the family. The crime and the reversed numbers represented her family's attack.

Randy had a difficult time finishing his doctoral disseration because of a dream in which he dropped dead while the academic hood was being placed over his head. On several occasions, his mother had said to him, "I'll be dead before you finish that!"

Guilt is passed from parents to patients when they decide to do something independent. The parents say in words, gesture, or tone of voice, "So, you don't want to take care of me anymore?" This guilt haunts patients with each independent move, in relation to taking care of their parents and other people.

There is a second part to this guilt-inducing parental message. It is a retaliation that frequently has a childlike quality. The parents say, "If you don't want to take care of me, I won't take care of you either!"

Dawn, a nurse, had invited her parents to visit and was supposed to meet them at the train station. She was delayed due to a medical emergency. Her parents did not wait, but instead took a taxi to her home. The next three times she flew home to spend a holiday with her family her parents failed to meet her at the airport because they were "too busy."

Patients have fairly reliable ways of responding to this parental accusation. They try to proceed with their plans and take care of others at the same time. This response is automatic.

Tracy was about to sign the papers that would enable her to buy a house. She postponed her meeting with the real estate agent. Instead, she stayed home to brood anxiously about whether to give parties for various members of her family.

Each patient has a different way of becoming separate. One patient, Lucille, chose to share with me a series of fantasies in which she returned to being a young child starting over again with a trusting relationship. She called it her "TV screen." Some of the images occurred spontaneously within her therapy hour, while others emerged between sessions and were reported during the following hour. Each fantasy represented progressive steps away from home into a new and trusting relationship with her therapist.

I am a grown woman in an astronaut's suit with many strings attached. I cut the strings and climb out of the suit. There are so many strings that the suit stands by itself! I feel very thin and nude and embarrassed. There is no place to hide. Someone hands me a pink bunting. I can't move much in it but it keeps me warm. [This fantasy expresses Lucille's fear of, and her sense of the aloneness in, stepping away from the commands into her own world. It also expresses her feeling that she has to start over again from the beginning like a baby.]
I am a young girl in outer space. It is black. I am standing on a huge metal disk with sharp, ragged edges. The rest of my family is cowering close together in the middle of the disc. I am standing on the edge. After much fear and deliberation, I jump off the disc. I don't know where I will land.
I float through black space and land in the middle of a patch of

plants called baby tears. There is an African violet in the middle. There is also a small pair of ladies' shoes. I look up to see a woman [whom she identifies as her therapist] wearing a suit. She is very tall and I feel very small. I can't see her head.

A woman is lying on the grass reading a newspaper. I am still a little girl, and I crawl in between her and the newspaper. We do not talk. I feel safe and happy.

The woman is very ill. She is in bed. I am about age ten now. I bring her a present and leave it on her bedside table. She does not wake up.

When I am a teenager the woman helps me to write something. She stands behind me pointing out necessary corrections. She encourages me to keep on writing. [This fantasy articulates Lucille's emerging ability to differentiate between supportive criticism and sabotage.]

For our psychotherapy hour I am in a rowboat in the middle of a small lake. You [the therapist] are on the dock. I stay out on the water. You wait for me to return. You don't leave the dock. You don't seem to mind. [This fantasy appears to represent for Lucille her emerging ability to be herself without wondering what other people would think. She is beginning to accept that she will not be abandoned.]

The woman in Lucille's fantasies was the symbol for her therapist. For Lucille, the fantasies represented working through. These fantasies were intermixed with other images representing the negative experiences in Lucille's childhood. She had to compare the two kinds of fantasies with each other and decide which one was really true of her relationship with me. My acceptance of the images allowed her to believe that she could have a positive relationship with me. She felt assured that her fantasies represented realistic wishes and needs.

GUIDING PATIENTS TOWARD INDEPENDENCE

When the therapy is successful, patients manage to find the courage to head out on their own. There is some practical information that therapists can give that will help the process along.

First, the myth of self-righteous perfection makes patients afraid to make mistakes. Instead of understanding errors as a necessary part of learning and living, they believe that mistakes signal an inability to manage; they are embarrassing and should be hidden or instantly corrected. To counter this misconception patients might be instructed to "be sure to make at least four mistakes between now and your next appointment."

Some patients naturally tend to cling to their relationship with their therapist. They discount their successes in life, hang onto problems, and demand special rescuing. These patients have come to believe that their self-esteem comes only from their parents, by being "special" or through receiving help. Such patients need the information that they can best build their self-esteem by mastering the problems of life, becoming independent, taking a risk, solving a problem for themselves, and feeling the pride that can come with success.

Impinged-upon adults do not view the anxiety that normally accompanies any new task as normal or as a universal experience. They have been taught that the feeling means "You can't do it; therefore, you should stop trying." These patients are surprised to learn that anxiety is simply a warning meaning "You are in new territory, so go slowly and be careful until you learn your way." They are pleased to learn that the anxiety will dissipate as the work of learning proceeds.

Therapists can encourage and model a sense of humor, which is another element almost always missing within an enmeshed family. Usually humor emerges as patients test their plans and strengthen their resistance to parental sabotage. Its emergence signals the appearance of an observing ego and the development of a whole self.

Andy paused a moment in his hour, reflected, and then started to say something that he felt was completely spontaneous and humorous. But he was uncomfortable and said, "Spontaneity means that I am not following the parental prescription. I am being myself. I am being bad."

This new sense of humor should not be confused with the defensive humor intended to sidetrack the therapist. An emerging sense of humor makes therapists laugh enjoyably, while a defensive sense of humor makes the therapist uncomfortable about consorting with the laughter.

In the course of psychotherapy, it often helps patients to

clarify the difference between getting constructive help with a life project and running back home for help within an enmeshed relationship to foster dependency. This difference was explained to one patient by using the following analogy.

Suppose that you are a Cub Scout about 7 years old. You seek appropriate help by going to the scout master and asking him how to tie a complex new knot. He shows you and you are now able to do it. Then you feel a strong urge to run home to Mother. She gives you one of those looks that says, "My, you have been gone a long time." You find yourself inviting her to help you to tie your shoe even though you learned to do that simple knot years ago. Your anxiety about your mother's discomfort with your progress in Scouts makes you act like you don't know how to tie your shoe.

Once patients begin to feel joy, they are often reluctant to "bother" therapists with their excitement. Joy means loss. Many patients say, "If I feel great, then you will respond by telling me to wind up the psychotherapy. If I feel ecstatic about what our relationship has been able to accomplish, then it will go away." There is a lot of work to do on this issue.

When patients are able to be joyful, it seems critical for the therapist to feel joy too. The patients are brave to share this new feeling openly. A therapeutic stance of neutrality can be devastating to this kind of patient since it is perceived by them as rejection or disinterest. The therapist needs to model excitement, curiosity, pleasure, relief, and humor, but in a manner that also maintains a proper degree of professional objectivity within the psychotherapeutic relationship.

Masterson (1976, 1981) speaks of the necessity of "communicative matching," or sharing in the details of the plans relating to a step forward. This form of help is a departure from a more traditional psychoanalytic approach. It seems a critical part of the work with impinged-upon adults.

When patients feel excessive pain, they may backtrack into the family symbiosis. They give their parents another chance to respond in a manner different from the way they always have before. The patients are usually disappointed.

At times the process seems like a catch-22. Impinged-upon

adults have to stop investing in the symbiotic relationship to be able to receive caring from other sources and build a separate person; it takes a whole, strong ego to handle all this, yet their ego is still in the building stages. Therapists need to keep in mind how far patients have come, the distance left to travel, and the goal.

DIFFICULT MOMENTS FOR THE PATIENT

The therapeutic relationship becomes important to patients. Patients want to believe that it is also an important relationship for the therapist.

Although patients do get to know therapists personally, they have to come to terms with the fact that the therapists may choose to present only the part of themselves necessary to effectively accomplish the therapeutic task. The patients are also able to present only a limited version of themselves through most of the psychotherapy because they do not yet feel like whole persons; usually that version is one of pseudocompliance or rebellion, developed as a style of functioning. One patient, Alice, wrote about this issue in her diary soon after a therapy hour.

My therapist has been what I need her to be, from a blank screen where I could discover my own thoughts, to lending me her ego when I had no idea what to do, to clarifying the misconceptions that have constrained my life. I've just come to realize that I don't really know who she is the way her friends do. She said that she felt privileged to do this work with me; but she has not allowed the relationship to become too important so that she can acknowledge my need to come and go. She told me something about her relationship with her students today. As I left the hour, my frustration mounted. I wanted to have the kind of relationship they had with her. I suddenly realized that I was not a whole person. I never had intimate connections within my own family. I was just a piece of a larger need. Now I find that, to become a whole person, I have many hours with someone who must limit what is presented with me. I lose the intimacy once more. Again I feel excluded. The only thing I can do is to face what I am not, so I can see what it is that I need to become. I must keep going because I know that there will be more for me.

Even harder is coming to terms with letting the real self emerge through movement toward an appropriate relationship, now possible, with the therapist. It is a frighteningly new relationship. Patients have to face the possibility that they will be totally rejected by their families, becoming psychologically orphaned. They can turn to friends, but friends are not the same as family, especially during holiday times. In addition, patients usually discover that many of the friendships that they thought important are also symbiotic. They have to be changed or relinquished. Patients must endure periods of feeling alone and avoid turning back to old pathological relationships for rescue.

One patient, Kendall, described the feelings that accompany this stage when reporting a dream.

She was leaving a concentration camp. She had found a way out, but realized that there was no way to go back in. Outside of the camp lay miles and miles of fields. She felt alone.

The existential separateness, after being taught that it does not exist, feels isolating. On the same day that Kendall reported this dream, she risked giving me a gift; the gift declared her commitment to, and appreciation for, her new therapeutic relationship.

After patients work through these feelings, a longing occurs for the missed events, relationships, and material things that would otherwise have been acquired. One patient felt it when she was walking down a street filled with beautiful homes. At middle age, she was single, living in a studio apartment. For the first time in her life, she wanted a home and family. The strength of this longing was uncomfortable. Another patient, who felt ambivalent about having a baby, visited a friend in the hospital who had just given birth. She reported the strong longing to have a baby of her own as different from the pain of not being a whole person. She saw the longing as a more positive kind of pain and was glad to feel it. It meant that she was on her way to getting a baby because her need was now clearly felt.

EXCITING MOMENTS FOR THE PATIENT

There are exciting realizations for patients. Some are subtle experiences, taken for granted or not noticed by others.

Impinged-upon adults get excited every time they take a new risk, disobey a command, and thereby find out that nothing terrible happens to them.

Arnold, after having set some limits with a friend, said, "The most gratifying thing in the world is to face a situation in which you have to say no, face the threatened abandonment, and find out that the rejection doesn't happen."

Patients feel surprised and delighted when they discover that someone *wants* to be with them, instead of abnormally *needing* them. They feel pleased to discover that relationships can be "straightforward and uncomplicated" rather than enmeshed with the commands. Patients derive a real sense of accomplishment when the therapist is unavoidably late for an appointment and they do not feel diminished by this event.

When their spouse leaves on a business trip, patients can feel exhilaration from the sense that they still exist as a whole person while the spouse is away. They are not just a piece of the marriage, fading away if their spouse is absent.

Achieving object constancy (discussed earlier) also brings a feeling of triumph and security. One patient, Cheryl, reported acquiring object constancy rather suddenly:

The detail was incredible. You had a soft look on your face, and you were wearing the same clothes you had on the last time I saw you. The image stayed with me all day. It was mine and I felt a triumph. I wanted to call and tell you about it. It was hard to go to sleep that night because of my excitement. It arrived just in time because you are going on vacation. Now I will have company while you are gone, and I can believe more fully that you will come back.

Patients feel a sense of mastery when psychosomatic symptoms (see Chapter 7) diminish. Even though these symptoms can be uncomfortable, patients may also feel a mild sense of loss because the physical symptoms act as intrapsychic parents stepping in to thwart the patients. Therefore, when the symptoms diminish, patients feel farther away from both real and intrapsychic parents. Since the patients are still searching for a new set of relationships, this sense of physical mastery is often accompanied by a feeling of loneliness.

Patients discover that feeling like a whole person is only one of a series of steps in the process of having meaningful relationships. As one patient, Ann, said,

> First I find myself. Then I want to see who I am! Once I begin to know that, then I want to see who I've married. Next, there are changes to make in the relationship. I want to assert more than I did before. It really makes me anxious to do all that. Again, I am still afraid of being left, of losing everything, to step out of my quiet security and complacency. It feels so good when I do, though. Now I can accept change as part of the relationship. ... I am fascinated with the differences between me and other people, not the sameness. I enjoy it as much as a color blind person might who sees color for the first time.

Each patient is proud of the courage that it took to face anxiety, go on, trust someone else, and let that person be different and significant. It is a relief to want to be alone without agitation, restlessness, and feeling incomplete. There is now the option to cancel work to take care of a sick child, go home for an evening and read a book, or not go out on Saturday night just because other people do.

PATIENTS RISK A RELATIONSHIP WITH THE THERAPIST

When impinged-upon adults have dealt with their intrapsychic parents, they feel some power and control and are less afraid to deal with their real parents. When patients feel like a separate person, they feel secure within their own boundaries and are more able to set limits and also to trust.

The stage is now set for the patients to focus on the relationship with the therapist. It is scary because expressing personal, intimate, or affectionate thoughts may seem to the patients that they are giving up those newly formed boundaries that make up a whole self.

Tim asked, "If I let you know that I like you, does that mean that you can come in and do anything you want to me?" His therapist explained that valuing him precluded her doing anything that would not support his growth. Tim responded, "Are people really like that?"

Toward the end of therapy, patients may wish to define and discuss the nature of the therapeutic relationship. Each relationship is unique. Patients who have worked very hard and shared pain and personal feelings may ask, "Can I love you?" "Do you love me?" They experience the relationship as a loving one.

Therapists will choose to answer this question in different ways. Some therapists feel that loving has no place in the therapeutic setting (Miller 1984). It would certainly not help patients for the therapist to attempt to replace the love missed in childhood or to substitute love for the working through of therapeutic issues. However, Freud said in a letter to Jung, "Psychoanalysis is in essence a cure through love" (Bettelheim 1982, p. iii). In the unique relationship of psychotherapy, therapists and patients may achieve aspects of the definition of love as defined in this book. They become two whole, separate persons who respect each other deeply. They share the development and expression of the patient's real self. However, the limits provided by the therapeutic relationship ensure that the relationship does not go beyond its stated therapeutic purpose.

WHAT IS LOVING SOMEONE ELSE?

Dan said to me, "My new girlfriend said that she was in love with me." He felt confused as to how to respond. He brought his dilemma into the therapy hour by saying, "What is love, anyway? Is it something that is supposed to come along and hit me between the eyes? I have experienced that. It feels like a head-on collision with someone else that is out of my control. Soon it runs into trouble. If that is what it is, I don't need it. I don't feel that with my girlfriend. I told her that I felt warm and happy when I was with her, and that I loved to talk with her, but I refuse to say I love her until I understand what that means. At least, I can be honest."

Lucinda thought love was "being totally open and honest, telling everything as if my life were an open book." Then she asked, "If my boyfriend refused to do that, does that mean that he doesn't love me?"

Both patients were referring to past experiences with symbiosis and current unresolved relationships. They felt a strong pull to be together, to be completely open (as if there were no separate boundaries), and to meet the other person's needs. The expected result is eventual unhappiness. Real loving is instead a commitment that builds much more slowly from a friendship, with much quality time and frequent, consistent interaction together.

OEDIPAL ISSUES

In many cases, the identification, analysis, and working through of maternal and paternal commands will be sufficient. However, there are a few cases in which an additional issue needs to be addressed. Patients may ultimately achieve some measure of autonomy, but something still stands in the way. The issue that blocks their exit from psychotherapy is often an oedipal one.

In the literature, therapists have argued that oedipal issues cannot exist until there is a sense of a separate self and the achievement of object constancy. If this is true, impinged-upon adults may have achieved just enough wholeness to deal with, and be affected by, both separation–individuation issues and oedipal issues concurrently.

Some parents are seductive and flirtatious as well as undermining. Their offspring are tantalized with the nonverbal invitation from the parent of the opposite sex to a sexual relationship that is never consummated unless there has been overt sexual abuse. These patients thus have an additional reason to stay home and strive for perfection: to win illusive forbidden sexual rewards and replace the parent of the same sex. These patients get stuck at the oedipal level trying to achieve the love in a sexual way they feel they never got as a younger child because of the enmeshment.

This issue comes up for both male and female patients. Some of them have stayed home for years, aborted college plans, or passed up dates to win a romantic relationship with the parent of the opposite sex. If they do manage to marry, they usually find a way to spoil it so that they can return home and remain romantically faithful to their parent.

Oedipal issues and enmeshment issues complement each other. A mother and a son have a relatively easy time setting up such a relationship when the father is in the background commanding that the son take psychological care of the mother. Maternal commands 2 and 3 serve to validate the oedipal issue.

If these romantic feelings are transferred to the therapist, the psychotherapy will be unduly prolonged unless this particular issue is confronted and worked through. Even when properly addressed, it often takes a long time to free patients to turn their romantic attention to a more available partner. Patients, who do not understand their romantic attachment to their therapist, have learned to wait tenaciously and indefinitely for their reward. The parents of such patients have done nothing to help the patients resolve this issue appropriately because the patients' romantic faithfulness is in the service of the enmeshed relationship. The patients are caught without being able to fulfill their needs for a loving and sexual partnership in life.

When patients do resolve the oedipal issue enough to have their own sexual partner, they tend to have nightmares about "killing" their opposite-sex parent and feel extremely guilty about abandonment. Thus, in the final analysis the patients return to the separation–individuation issue.

The following dialogue is an example of separation and oedipal issues occurring within the same therapy hour.

Dan, an older banker, began his therapy hour by saying that his mother had telephoned to inform him that she would be coming to see his new house. He had not given any response because he hadn't known what to say. In the first part of the hour, he addressed separation issues:

"I resented not being asked. I resented that she did not even consider that I might not want her to come. She has never seen where I live, and I don't want her to see it because she will be critical and sabotaging of the life that I have built for myself. . . . I feel like I would be taking care of her, and I don't want to do that for more than a long weekend."

Next he turned to oedipal feelings:

"But in a way, I do want her to come. I am afraid that she will like everything I have done and then I will feel strangely disappointed and angry with her for doing that. I would want to pick a fight with her. If she liked everything about my life, I would take that to mean that she didn't really want me to come back home and be the center of her life. . . . I feel really confused. I guess there is no right way for Mother to be with me. Maybe I do want her to visit. At least that will give me fresh information to figure this out."

The enmeshment issue must be dealt with first, followed by the emergence of the oedipal issues. For a time, the issues intermingle because parents will often use the myth of self-righteous perfection to lure patients into a romantic relationship that can never be really satisfying. These patients are encouraged to think of themselves as special, as somebody perfect — as long as they stay home with the parent of the opposite sex. The implicit message is that if perfection is achieved, the reward will be sexual union. The patients strive for the perfection but never obtain the sexual union. This leaves patients extremely confused about who they really are.

Laurie was considering a new dating relationship instead of continuing to battle the oedipal issues with her father. She described her new boyfriend as handsome and "the kindest person" she had ever known. Yet she doubted the value of any relationship because "no one was perfect."

I presented the following analogy to Laurie: "It is as if you had been climbing a mountain all of your life. It is so high that the top has always been in the clouds, but you are determined to get there [oedipal union with her father]. You come to me [the therapist], and I challenge your climb and invite you to consider staying in one of the beautiful valleys [boyfriend]. You like the valley but it is not perfect. You keep looking over your shoulder at the top of the mountain. You've even considered climbing the neighboring peak (transferential relationship with me). You are reluctant to give up that climb."

Laurie strongly confirmed my analogy and added, after a pause, "It would be so nice to think that I didn't have to make it to the top. It has taken so much time and energy. Yet, I've gone this far; it is hard to give up." I inquired, "What is getting to the top?" Laurie replied, "I can't see it clearly; as you say, it is in the clouds, but I think it means being crowned the most special, like a queen, getting to live a romantic perfect life where I am taken care of."

After considerable working through of this issue, and after she had been dating a man she was very fond of, Laurie reported the following dream: "I was climbing up a vine on the outside of my father's house to his bedroom on the third floor [oedipal conquest]. My boyfriend was climbing with me. When I got to the window, my father refused to let me in [abandonment]. I was faced with climbing down again. I was very scared."

Laurie was on her way to facing abandonment from her father and resolving both her separation–individuation conflict and her oedipal conflict.

CHAPTER 10

Supporting Literature

THE DIAGNOSIS OF BORDERLINE

For many years the term *borderline* has been a catchword diagnosis in psychiatry and clinical psychology, describing a wide range of people who appear to be suffering from neither neurotic nor psychotic processes. There has been a flood of articles and books attempting to describe this kind of personality organization and to create a form of effective treatment (Balint 1968, Boyer and Giovacchini 1967, Chatham 1985, Giovacchini 1984, 1986, Grinker and Werble 1977, Grotstein 1981, Hedges 1983, Kernberg 1980, 1984, Masterson 1972, 1976, 1981, 1983, 1985, Masterson and Rinsley 1975, Miller 1981, Rinsley 1981, 1982, 1984, 1985, Searles 1986, Stone 1980, 1986). The existing literature is replete with controversy regarding both diagnosis and treatment. There have been countless attempts to review the literature of the borderline. It is not necessary to repeat this exhaustive task here (Chatham 1985, Hedges 1983, Masterson 1976, Rinsley 1982, Stone 1980, 1986). Instead, a few brief coments on some of the literature that has influenced the development of the ideas presented in this book will suffice.

Part of the difficulty in agreeing upon a defining set of characteristics and a treatment plan appears to be that mental health professionals are talking about a wide range of functioning within the broad rubric *borderline,* that necessitates flexibility in treatment approaches.

Hedges (1983) speaks to the same issue:

> Borderline developmental limitations do not lend themselves to categorizations by "symptom" or "syndromes" because the array of behavioral and dynamic possibilities is literally infinite since the ways a child reacts to mothering are infinite.
>
> Reluctance [by baby] to relinquish the immediacy of the dyadic experience in favor of separation and individuation results in highly idiosyncratic developmental arrests which subsequently undergo a series of adaptive convolutions. The specific area(s) of arrested development, depending on how crucial or how pervasive they are, may have only minor consequences for future development of the child or may have massive implications for development. [pp. 134–35]

Despite these obvious complexities within the profession of psychology and psychiatry, theorists and clinicians have now generally agreed upon certain characteristics describing borderline functioning (Grinker and Werble 1977, Gunderson and Singer 1975, Kernberg 1980, 1984, Masterson 1976, 1981, Rinsley 1982, Stone 1986):

1. A superficially high degree of sociability coupled with difficulty being alone.
2. Unstable interpersonal relationships.
3. Instability because they see themselves and the world in terms of extremes of good and bad.
4. The predominance of anger and depression.
5. Anhedonia, or an inability to feel and enjoy pleasure.
6. A poorly developed sense of self.
7. Impaired achievement in completing the life steps of profession, marriage, and family.
8. Unusual access to creativity, although they may have difficulty organizing it.
9. Self-destructive behavior, including self-mutilation.
10. Drug and alcohol abuse.
11. Sexual promiscuity and confusion.

12. Brief psychotic episodes.

13. Primitive ecstatic experiences, such as being drunk or "high."

Additionally, some theorists have attempted to create discernible subtypes within the broader category of borderline. Experts such as Kernberg, Masterson, and Rinsley speak at workshops and conferences of "higher-level" borderline and "lower-level" borderline.

The first eight characteristics seem to fit the higher-level borderline, or persons who are functioning closer to the neurotic level. These patients are motivated to seek treatment, keep their appointments regularly, and are relatively consistent in the behavior they manifest. They are seeking out psychotherapy in increasing numbers and are achieving successful results with once- or twice-weekly outpatient treatment. The patients who have provided vignettes for this book are higher-level borderline.

A relatively high percentage of such patients demonstrate disciplined, successful, and integrated creativity in music, poetry, and writing. Creativity appears to be born out of internal conflict and the borderline's greater access to the layer of experience where primitive thoughts and emotions reside (Balint 1968, Sass 1982). Many of these patients show "special faculties and particular ways of reacting both to internal and external milieu that make possible the expression of the creative urge" (Giovacchini 1986, p. 430).

The remaining five characteristics seem to more adequately describe the lower-level borderline, whose functioning is closer to psychotic. These patients demonstrate unpredictable behavior and often require treatment in a hospital setting. Most of the literature about the borderline is actually about the lower level borderline or hospitalized patients (Boyer and Giovacchini 1967, Giovacchini 1984, Kernberg 1984, Searles 1986, Stone 1986).

Some estimates indicate that the borderline personality represents 10 percent of the population and 25 percent of the patients in treatment (Sass 1982). Searles (1986) seems correct in suggesting that the borderline population is probably much larger:

> I have found that there is no lack of borderline psychopathology among . . . highly qualified and effective persons. Another way of putting it is that I know that I am far from alone, among mental health professionals, in carrying around my own share of proclivity for the use of borderline defenses. [p. xii]

THE NATURE AND ORIGIN OF THE BORDERLINE PSYCHOPATHOLOGY

There are two developmental tasks that young children should accomplish during the preoedipal period. The first is to develop a sense of separateness from significant caretakers. The second task is to develop a sense of constancy or feeling of integration and unity regarding both self and others. The literature supports the thesis within this book that the borderline patients have difficulty with these tasks because their parents' psychological needs have prevented them from developing independent and separate selves (Brown 1986, Chernin 1985, Masterson 1976, Peck 1978, 1983, Rinsley 1982). Instead, the parent has, in unconscious ways, sabotaged the borderline patients' growth by threatening them with the loss of the relationship whenever they take a step away from the family. Therefore, to avoid abandonment, children remain enmeshed or symbiotically attached as an extension of their parents and fail to develop autonomous separate selves (Masterson 1976, 1981, Rinsley 1982).

As a result of this difficulty in parental relationships, borderline patients do not grow out of the primitive defense of splitting and fail to integrate the good and bad experiences of self and others. Therefore, their sense of self-identity and their perception of others tend to fluctuate from moment to moment according to their unintegrated perceptions.

Borderline patients have not achieved a stable sense of object constancy. Kaplan (1978) speaks of the necessity of object constancy for effective interpersonal relationships:

> Our emotional acceptance of the idea that we are neither saints nor demons but whole persons who are capable of ordinary human love and ordinary human hatred. By uniting our loving emotions with our emotions of anger and hatred, constancy confirms our sense of personal wholeness. . . . When constancy is weak, the only way to protect the

cherished parts is to split them apart and to keep them fenced off. When the good and the bad are split apart, the wholeness of the self fragments and disintegrates. And then it becomes impossible to appreciate and respect the wholeness of others. [p. 30]

Much theoretical work has centered on trying to locate a stage of development in which borderline difficulties begin, in an effort to identify a fixation point. Masterson (1976) and Rinsley (1982) believe that the problem begins very early in infancy and reaches a peak in the period of 16 to 36 months.

As Giovacchini (1986) and Chatham (1985) have argued, it is not particularly useful to declare a fixation point because parents' failure to allow the child to become a separate person starts at the beginning of the child's life and continues indefinitely until the child interrupts the process. As Chatham (1985) says,

> The therapist should avoid hunting for the "right stage" . . . [because] borderline adults regularly reveal distortions that arose from more than one stage. These distortions, after all, are influenced by the previous stage. Early developmental pathologic problems are played out again in the Oedipal period, with perhaps a subsequent distorting of this process, and yet again during the second individuation process that occurs in adolescence. [p. 159]

UNDERSTANDING THE PATIENTS' PARENTS

In his best seller, *People of the Lie,* Peck (1983) recommends that psychiatry recognize a new personality disorder called *evil.* Although the word *evil* may be too pejorative and connotative of religion to be clinically useful to patients examining their parental relationships, Peck's criteria are useful in describing the parents of borderline patients:

1. Consistent destructive, scapegoating behavior, which may often be quite subtle.
2. Excessive, albeit usually covert, intolerance to criticism and other forms of narcissistic injury.
3. Pronounced concern with a public image and self-image of respectability, contributing to a stability of life-style but also to pretentiousness and denial of hateful feelings or vengeful motives.

> 4. Intellectual deviousness, with increased likelihood of a mild schizophrenic-like disturbance of thinking at times of stress. [p. 129]

Peck then speaks poignantly regarding the task that the children of such parents face.

> If evil were easy to recognize, identify, and manage there would be no need for this book. But the fact of the matter is that it is the most difficult of all things with which to cope. If we, as objectively detached mature adults, have great difficulty coming to terms with evil, think what it must be like for the child living in its midst.
>
> To come to terms with evil in one's parentage is perhaps the most difficult and painful psychological task a human being can be called upon to face. Most fail and so remain its victims. [p. 130]

Brown (1986) speaks of the same kind of parenting but chooses to use the softer phrase "innocent evil" or "the unintentional thwarting of the growth and independence of the child" (p. 115). Coincidentally, in this book she uses the analogy of a broken leg with a slightly different emphasis. She describes a parent with a crippled leg threatening death if the child does not take the crippled leg and give the parent the child's healthy one. "So both parent and child then hobble along together. Neither becomes whole" (p. 31).

A patient, Marie Cardinal (1983), in recounting her analysis speaks of the relationship with her mother from the patient's point of view.

> What can even a willful child do in the face of an impervious, seductive, secretly crazy adult who is, furthermore, her own mother? Hide as much as possible her falcon feathers, transforming herself into a dove in order to preserve her true nature. I had played the game so early and so long that I had forgotten my appetite for competition, for victory and freedom. I had believed I was a dutiful daughter and I was a rebel. I had been one from birth. I existed. . . . There was in me an independence, a pride, a curiosity, a sense of justice and pleasure which didn't square with the role which fell to me in the society of my family. [p. 200]

All caretakers inevitably fail their children in some respects. However, it is important to say that deficiencies in the ability to love and parent stem primarily from psychological limitations within the parent rather than from intentional malice. It is also important to note that some children come into the world with difficult personalities (Gardner 1985). Thus, "internal object relations, concerning both 'bad' and 'good objects' are generated out of the intensity of infantile passions as well as parental character pathology" (Mitchell 1981, p. 396). Therapists do better psychotherapy when we approach origins of psychological difficulty in terms of accountability without blame.

THEORETICAL FRAMES OF REFERENCE

Object Relations Theory

The object relations theory focuses on the earliest stage of life, when children acquire an awareness of the difference between the self and others in their external world and achieve a basic sense of object constancy. The ideas presented in this book are more closely related to this theory than to any other.

Similar conclusions reached separately by Masterson and Rinsley and first published in 1975 concerning the role of mothers in the psychological development of their children seem to explain the tendency of patients to sabotage repeatedly their own steps forward. The most valuable part of Rinsley and Masterson's approach encompasses their explanation of mothers' need to reward for regression and threaten abandonment for growth, and their children's resulting abandonment depression (Masterson 1976, Rinsley 1982). Rinsley (1984) describes the "push–pull" conflict:

> What is discovered in the case of the borderline personality is a maternal injunction to the effect that to grow up is to face the calamitous loss or withdrawal of maternal supplies, coupled with the related injunction that to avoid that calamity, the child must remain dependent, inadequate, symbiotic–the depersonifying "push-pull" tie that binds. [p. 5–6]

In terms of the Masterson–Rinsley approach, I have developed my own vocabulary of *commands* and *permissions* that details the specific ways in which parental sabotage is carried out and encompasses both parental rewarding and abandoning behavior.

Masterson (1983) advises confrontation as the primary intervention for borderline patients whenever they are unable to do the psychotherapy work themselves. This intervention avoids rescuing patients who are already used to having their parents do for them. This advice to therapists seems sound but occasionally limiting, if the total reparenting needs of patients of this kind are considered. Sometimes patients stop the therapeutic work for reasons other than a wish to be rescued. Overuse of confrontation can lead to an hour that lacks richness and focus (Masterson 1983). Contributions from other theorists, explained in the following sections, provide a wider range of options in treating borderline patients.

The work of Bowlby (1969, 1973, 1980) explains the affect and behavior that accompanies separation and loss. Kaplan (1978), Kernberg (1972), Mahler (1974, 1975), and Winnicott (1965) provide an understanding of the infants' normal developmental process. Gould (1978), Sheehy (1976, 1981), and Vaillant (1977) shed light on the stages of development that borderline patients are missing. My creation of the permissions represents a condensation of this knowledge.

Family Research and Therapy

There is a considerable body of research on family dynamics, family therapy, and the etiology of schizophrenia that has been helpful and validating in the conceptualization of this book (Nichols 1984). In recent years object relations theorists and family therapists have been sharing overlapping concepts (Slipp 1984).

Bateson and colleagues (1956) introduced the concept of the *double-bind*. In this situation patients have a relationship with a significant other where a response is mandatory and escape is not possible. They receive two contradictory but related messages, usually at two different levels in a subtle manner in which it is difficult to realize the inconsistency. A double-bind, not to be confused with simple contradiction, has six characteristics:

1.   Two or more persons are involved in an important relationship.

2. The relationship is a repeated experience.

3. A primary negative injunction is given.

4. A second injunction, often nonverbal, is given that conflicts with the first, also enforced by punishment.

5. A third injunction is given that demands a response and prohibits escape (necessary part of the bind).

6. Once the victim is conditioned, any part of the double-bind is enough to evoke rage or panic.

In the case examples within this book, the permissions and commands are delivered simultaneously as contradictory injunctions with many of the elements of the double-bind.

Two other concepts come from the work of Wynne's study of schizophrenic families (Wynne et al. 1958). He introduced the concept of *pseudomutuality*, or the family facade that gives the impression that family members have good relationships. They present an image of fitting together so uniformly that there is no room for separate identities or differences of opinion. Their pseudomutuality keeps conflicts and intimacy from emerging. The second of Wynne's concepts is that of the *rubber fence*. The rubber fence is employed to keep family members from gaining separateness. It is an invisible barrier that precludes any meaningful contact outside the family. It may be stretched to allow such activities as going to school or work, but it pulls back hard if the involvement goes too far. The members of the family most in need of outside help are the ones most restricted. Bizarre behavior on the part of patients may be the only way to get around these restrictions, but such behavior evokes total rejection by the family so that pseudomutuality can be restored.

These two concepts are similar to the myth of self-sufficiency, the myth of perfection, and mother commands 1, 2, 3, 8, 9, and 10 set forth in preceding chapters in this book. However, since I was not acquainted with Wynne's concepts until after I created the commands, permissions, and myths, my work may be regarded as an independent corroboration.

A fourth concept is Lidz's *marital skew* (1973), in which there is serious psychopathology in one marital partner who dominates the other. This is the most frequent manner in which patients' parents accommodate each other's psychological needs.

Although Lidz has written primarily about schizophrenia, the same but less severe family dynamics seem to create the borderline condition. As Lidz has suggested, both schizophrenia and borderline disorders appear to orginate in the interpersonal relationships within the family. The pattern of psychopathological interaction can be defined, and improvements within the family can be satisfactorily made. His definition of parental sabotage is similar to that of Rinsley (1982, 1984) and Masterson (1976).

Transactional Analysis

Like Berne (1961, 1974), I like to draw from fictional and nonfictional literature as one way of understanding human interaction. I like to speak in modern, updated, simple terms understandable to both patients and therapists. Berne speaks about the broad "scripts" for life that children receive from their parents by the age of 6, whereas I speak of many different parental messages. Both of us hold an optimistic view that patients can actively change their situation. Berne writes with a sense of humor and with a gimmickry that is not present in this book, however. On the contrary, some of the commands evoke a quiet and serious mood in many people.

Psychoanalytic and Psychodynamic Theory

I am indebted to Kaiser's book *Effective Psychotherapy* (1965). His chapter entitled "Emergency" highlights the valuable and respectful interchange of learning between patients and therapists. Kaiser's book provoked my early thinking regarding the issues of inappropriate fusion, separateness, aloneness, and responsibility. He defines the patient's fundamental problem as the *universal symptom*: the attempt to achieve the delusion of fusion (to incorporate him- or herself into another person and lose one's own personality, or to incorporate and destroy the other person's personality). Kaiser (1965) defines the *universal conflict* as stemming from the reality of separateness and aloneness.

Closeness as it is accessible for an adult illuminates more than anything else could the unbridgeable gap between two individuals and underlies the fact that nobody can get rid of the full responsibility for his own words and actions. [p. xix]

He sees therapy as "an attitude on the part of the therapist which emanates naturally from his interest in making possible a relationship where the equality and the autonomy of the patient are respected" (Kaiser 1965, p. xvi).

My relationships with patients have also been influenced by the work of Sullivan (1956) and Chapman (1978). His approach to psychotherapy is based on observable human relationships, with the sole purpose of psychotherapy being to help patients to become aware of interpersonal relationships and their concomitant feelings and thoughts. This is accomplished by dialogues in which patients and therapists actively work together, speaking without psychological jargon. Sullivan's concept of *parataxic distortion* appears to be a broader and therefore more effective concept for borderline patients than Freud's concept of transference. Parataxic distortion is not just the reliving of a past relationship within the therapeutic relationship; it is the "repeating of a pattern of feeling and behavior developed gradually during the formative years" (Chapman 1978, p. 116).

In addition, the works of Angyal (1965), Greban (1984), Miller (1984), and Taft (1962) have encouraged me to provide a real relationship for patients in addition to the working alliance.

Short-term Therapy

My study and teaching of short-term therapy techniques (Davanloo 1978, Mann 1973, Small 1979, Wolberg 1980) has influenced me to consolidate a central focus for borderline patients. The short-term therapy model highlights and actively works out the central issue. This model forces therapists to consider the ways in which therapists and patients can interact with each other around issues of dependency, therapeutic ritual, and laziness. The short-term therapy and life stages are both finite, highlighting the need to provide help as speedily as possible to borderline patients, who have already lost so much time in the service of their parents.

The short-term therapy model sanctions giving advice for the purpose of expanding patients' range of possible choices once the resistance and the historical material have been worked through.

TREATMENT CONSIDERATIONS

Mental health professionals have recommended a wide range of treatment options:

1. No treatment because borderline patients are untreatable, certainly unsuitable for psychoanalysis.
2. Medication for depression and variable behavior.
3. Hospitalization to curb the self-destructive behavior of the lower-level borderline (Masterson 1972, Rinsley 1982).
4. Supportive therapy (Masterson 1976, 1981).
5. Long-term intensive treatment (Giovacchini 1984, Masterson 1972).
6. Once- to twice-weekly out-patient confrontational treatment (Masterson 1972).
7. Short-term focused treatment (Davanloo 1978, Mann 1973, Small 1979, Wolberg 1980).
8. Individual therapy in conjunction with family therapy (Lidz 1973).

Higher-level borderline patients can definitely benefit from a once- to twice-weekly time-limited psychotherapy of one to two years' work with a clearly understood focus on commands, permissions, myths, and general knowledge concerning separation–individuation issues. In addition, successful therapy requires that therapists hold two basic assumptions:

1. It is the mental health professionals' responsibility to provide a supportive response to growth to replace the inadequacies of parenting at various developmental subphases.

Some basic form of real, honest, direct relationship is required that has the components of reparenting.

2. Patients are the only ones to assume responsibility for their present limitations and future plans unless they are acting dangerously toward themselves or others. Therapists must always respect and expect patients to take on this responsibility. This attitude of respect is one of the cornerstones supporting growth and creates a reality around which patients' behavior can be examined, evaluated, confronted, and supported (Masterson 1972, 1976).

THE BORDERLINE DILEMMA IN LITERATURE AND THE ARTS

Issues of separation and individuation are now appearing regularly in popular literature, magazines (Sass 1982), and television, indicating the public's need for a greater understanding of separation–individuation issues.

Mr. Rogers' Neighborhood aired a fascinating presentation surrounding the issue of separation and independence for the preschool audience. A policeman in the "land of make-believe" wanted to leave the town to go away to study opera. Another character tried to prevent his departure by surrounding him with a large paper chain. The policeman breaks the chain and explains that trying to hold someone back will not enhance but only hurt the relationship. If instead he is allowed to go freely, he will return with his new talent to entertain the community from time to time. The community then expresses their sadness at his departure but allows him to leave freely.

The popular dramatization of *Brideshead Revisited* by Evelyn Waugh (1945) studies the gradual demise of an attractive young man, Sebastian, whose life was constantly directed for him by his mother to benefit her psychological needs. Lady Marchmain is a skillfully drawn character who masks her inner turmoil with iron control, unbending manipulative demands, extreme propriety, and a total absence of love. Sebastian's most supportive companion is his teddy bear. Sebastian ends up as a drunken derelict in North Africa having achieved only a physical distance from his family.

Anne Tyler's novels, such as *Dinner at the Homesick Restaurant* (1982), are filled with characters attempting to make a separation from family. Ben Joe, in *If Morning Ever Comes*, is a young man in college who "can't seem to get anywhere, nowhere permanent" (Tyler 1964, p. 43) from a family who "were a set of square dancers coming to clap the palms of their hands to each other only their hands missed by inches and encountered nothing" (p. 20).

Ben Joe leaves college to return home for a visit to see his family. Anne Tyler writes about his call to his mother to ask permission to return home, and describes a beautiful example of his lack of object constancy.

> Ben Joe waited, frowning into the receiver, twining the coils of the telephone cord around his index finger. He tried desperately to picture what she looked like right now, but all he came up with was her hair, dust-colored with the curls at the side of her face pressed flat by the receiver. That was no help. Give him anything—eyes, mouth, just a stretch of cheek, even—and he could tell something, but not hair, for goodness' sake. He tried again. [p. 17]

Superficially, his mother frowns upon his need to return home, but Ben Joe also understands her nonverbal underlying communication rewarding his dependency.

> Ben Joe shrugged and pulled his pillow up behind him so that he could sit against it. The sheets smelled crisp and newly ironed; his mother had smoothed them tight on the bed herself and turned the covers down for him, and he could hold that thought securely in his mind even when she scolded him for returning. You had to be a sort of detective with his mother; you had to search out the fresh-made bed, the flowers on the bureau, and the dinner table laid matter-of-factly with your favorite supper, and then you forgot her crisp manners. Ben Joe was still watching mother with those detective eyes even though he was a grown man and should have stopped bothering. [p. 54]

Finally, the self-help literature is also aiding people with borderline problems. *August* (Rossner 1983), *My Mother, My Self* (Friday 1977), and *Mommie Dearest* (Crawford 1978) are best sellers. The popular *Women Who Love Too Much* by Norwood (1985) describes fifteen characteristics of women who stay too long in dysfunctional relationships. Eight of these examples are characteristic of the patients described in this book.

1. Having received little real nurturing yourself, you try to fill this unmet need vicariously by becoming a care-giver, especially to men who appear in some way needy.
2. Because you were never able to change your parent(s) into the warm, loving caretaker(s) you longed for, you respond deeply to the familiar type of emotionally unavailable man whom you can try to change, through your love.
3. Terrified of abandonment, you will do anything to keep the relationship from dissolving.
4. Accustomed to lack of love in personal relationships, you are willing to wait, hope, and try harder to please.
5. You are willing to take far more than 50 percent of the responsibility, guilt, and blame in the relationship.
6. Your self-esteem is critically low, and deep inside you do not believe you deserve to be happy. Rather, you believe you must earn the right to enjoy life.
7. By being drawn to people with problems that need fixing or by being enmeshed in situations that are chaotic, uncertain, and emotionally painful, you avoid focusing on your responsibility to yourself.
8. You are not attracted to men who are kind, stable, reliable, and interested in you. You find such "nice" men boring. [Norwood 1985, pp. 10–11]

I Only Want What's Best for You by Brown (1986) speaks clearly to parents about not using their children to solve their emotional problems, and Halpern's *Cutting Loose* (1976) and *How to Break Your Addiction to a Person* (1982) are self-help guides for adults about becoming independent both from their parents and from dysfunctional love relationships. Lerner (1985) addresses ways in which women can use anger to effect a separation from the behavioral problems of significant others.

Public Television's *Masterpiece Theatre* aired D. H. Lawrence's *Sons and Lovers*, originally written in 1913. The story of Paul Morel's strong tie to his mother is said to parallel Lawrence's own experience. The last page of the novel details Morel's confusion yet determination to separate psychologically from his dead mother. He had just left his lover.

There was no Time, only Space. Who could say that his mother had lived or did not live? She had been in one place, and was in another, that was all. And his soul could not leave her, wherever she was. Now she had gone abroad into the night, and he was with her still. They were together. But yet there was his body, his chest, that leaned against the stile, his hands on the wooden bar. They seemed something. Where was he? . . . She was the only thing that held him up, himself, amid all this. And she was gone, intermingled herself. He wanted her to touch him, have him alongside with her.

But no, he would not give in. Turning sharply, he walked towards the city's phosphorescence. His fists were shut, his mouth set fast. He would not take that direction, to the darkness, to follow her. He walked towards the faintly humming, glowing town, quickly. [p. 420]

The ending leaves one feeling sad because Morel, despite his determination, did not have the necessary understanding and working-through of his emotions to break away.

ADDITIONAL WAYS TO STUDY THE BORDERLINE PATIENT

Theorists and clinicians are often guilty of speaking about the borderline population in impersonal, theoretical, pejorative, condescending, and overly dramatic terms. Perhaps this is a way of releasing feelings about a too wide continuum of patients who have been baffling, variable, and frustrating to treat because there is not a sufficient frame of reference from which to respond to them (Johnson 1985, Reiser and Levenson 1984).

For a time, during my ongoing study of the borderline patient, I decided to stop reading and just listen to my patients and record and study what they told me. Out of this experience came a clear frame of reference—the subject of this book—from which to respond to their dialogue with me. This respectful stance with them, not so surprisingly, aided the psychotherapy process.

It is admittedly difficult to make valid inferences about childhood from adult behavior. Since it is not possible to go back and research the childhood of adult patients, it is necessary to listen, share, and learn from material contributed by patients themselves (with, of course, the patients' permission). The works of Brown (1986), Cardinal (1983), Lindner (1955), Norwood (1985), and Yalom and Elkin (1974) have provided valuable information from the patients' perspective to therapists' accumulated knowledge.

We have preferred to write about the borderline condition from an adult perspective. However, there are borderline children currently seeking therapy with separation and individuation problems. Gardner (1985) in *Separation Anxiety Disorder* writes about school-phobic children. His description of the parents and the psychodynamics correlates very closely with the material in this book. The children and their families currently seeking therapy will become a rich source of additional information for therapists' clinical understanding.

THE SOCIETAL CONTRIBUTION TO BORDERLINE PSYCHOPATHOLOGY

To understand the borderline dilemma, it seems necessary to consider societal changes, especially for women, as a contributing factor in the development of borderline pathology. Authors of articles in popular magazines speculate about whether the lack of a nuclear family or the greater number of professional choices for women are contributing factors in the borderline problem (Sass 1982).

Many patients currently in treatment have parents who reached maturity during the Second World War. The men went off to fight leaving the women as single parents and as occupants of the jobs that the men vacated. Many women were suddenly presented with work opportunities previously denied them. They thrived under these new, temporary circumstances and came away from the experience with a new sense of their "professional" definition. At the same time, psychologists began articulating early developmental stages, the developmental aspects of intelligence, and the importance of mothers' staying at home. Society designed more organized ways for mothers to be involved with their children. Those who continued in, or returned to, full-time homemaking may have wished that their "career" as parents could last longer. They were not ready to retire after eighteen to twenty years, especially when jobs for women were not yet plentiful. Perhaps some mothers vicariously lived through their children and unconsciously found ways to keep their children dependent for a longer period of time. Many patients speak sympathetically of intelligent mothers who never got to do what they really wanted in terms of a career.

In the 1980s, many young women have established a professional career before starting their families. They have been given the chance to experience mastery and build their own sense of identity in a way that is separate from the career of parenting their children. It is therefore less painful for working mothers to have their children leave home because their careers and identities as professionals will continue.

Some of the children of the eighties have, and will, become "latch-key kids," growing up with a new problem called neglect, until society learns to accommodate women with good child care on the job site, leaves of absence, and adjusted work schedules to accommodate both raising children and working. Many of these children are having to separate too early, assuming adult responsibility in caring for themselves while their parents are at work.

Affirming Changes of Growth

The material presented in this book has been organized with the criteria for a good theory proposed by Haley in *Beyond the Double Bind*. By his definition, a good theory should comprehensively and clearly articulate the causes of failure, the components of healthy functioning, and the actions required of therapists to promote realistic hope and a successful outcome. The presenting problems articulate patients' sense of failure and confusion, and the commands explain their lack of growth. The permissions delineate the components of healthy functioning. The later chapters define the actions required of both patients and therapists.

When patients are ready to graduate from the therapeutic relationship, the five statements articulating the presenting problem are now replaced with the following conclusions, which represent the working through to understanding and the resultant healthy functioning:

1. My parents and I had a psychopathologically symbiotic relationship in which we rescued each other for the purpose of maintaining a mutual psychological dependency. I will never be able to take responsibility for their psychological needs. I had a right to feel angry about the impinging nature of our relationship, but now I can feel some compassion and forgiveness for

their psychological vulnerability and my resulting complementary limitations.

2. I now understand that my parents became unhappy with my progress because they could see my growth only as an abandonment of them. The more I accomplish, the more pain they will feel until I satisfactorily separate from them. Then they may be able to feel limited pride. I must learn to validate myself for the work I have done.

3. I was taught not to express anger at my parents directly. Therefore, I could only express my anger indirectly by refusing to act in ways that I thought would allow my parents to feel proud of me, even if that meant blocking my own progress.

4. I have been so busy caring for my parents' psychological incompleteness that I have little motivation for my own life. Also, I feared consequences to them and myself if I went on with my life.

5. I now understand that I am entitled to my own separate existence. My parents must assume responsibility for their psychological incompleteness. They will not die, and neither will I. I have been conditioned to feel anxious about going on with life, but I will no longer let this feeling impede my growth. I leave home as a separate and different individual. I see my parents as more capable than they let on to improve the quality of their own life without me. I believe they will benefit psychologically from my departure.

Glossary

Clarification: those dialogues between patients and therapists that bring the psychological phenomenon being examined into sharp focus. The significant details are highlighted and carefully separated from the extraneous material.

Entitlement: rights given at birth to decide what to do and what to share or withhold.

False self: the patient's facade of compliance and accommodation created in response to an environment that ignores the patient's needs and feelings. The patient withholds a secret real self that is unrelated to external reality (Hedges 1983).

Impingement: the obliteration of psychological and sometimes physical separation between individuals without obtaining permission.

Insight: the ability to perceive and understand a new aspect of mental functioning or behavior.

Interpretation: the therapist's verbalizing to patients in a meaningful, insightful way material previously unconscious to them (Langs 1973).

Introjection: the taking into oneself, in whole or in part, attributes from another person (Chatham 1985).

Object: a psychoanalytic term used to represent another person, animal, or important inanimate object (Chatham 1985).

Object constancy: the ability to evoke a stable, consistent memory of another person when that person is not present, irrespective of frustration or satisfaction (Masterson 1976).

Object relations theory: a theory that focuses on the earliest stages of life when children become aware of the difference between the self and the external world. This theory describes accompanying developmental tasks and also explains the difficulties that result if these tasks are incompletely accomplished.

Observing ego: the ability to stand outside oneself and look at one's own behavior.

Oedipal: a stage of childhood development that begins at about 3 years of age. After a stable differentiation of self, mother, and father has been achieved, children engage in a triangular relationship with their parents that includes love and rivalry.

Preoedipal: the period of early childhood development, ages 0 to 2, which occurs before the oedipal period. The developmental issues are the formation of constant internal memory of others and a separate sense of self.

Projective identification: fantasies of unwanted aspects of the self are deposited into another person, and then recovered in a modified version (Ogden 1979).

Reframing: the therapist's description, from a different perspective, of an event in the patient's life, providing new insight.

Separation–individuation: separation includes disengagement from mother and the creation of separate boundaries, with recognition of differences between mother and self. Individuation is ongoing achievement of a coherent and meaningful sense of self created through development of psychological, intellectual, social, and adaptive coping (Chatham 1985, Rinsley 1985).

Splitting: the holding apart of two opposite, unintegrated views of the self or another person, resulting in a view that is either all good and nurturing or all bad and frustrating. There is no integration of good and bad (Johnson 1985).

Symbiosis: an interdependent relationship between self and another in which the energies of both partners are required for the survival of self and other (Masterson 1976).

Transference: the inappropriate transfer of problems and feelings from past relationships to present relationships (Chatham 1985).

Transitional object: a soft or cuddly object an infant holds close as a substitute for contact with mother when she is not present. A transitional object aids in the process of holding on and letting go and provides soothing qualities. It represents simultaneously an extension of self and mother (Chatham 1985).

Working through: the second phase of therapy involving the investigation of origins of anger and depression through transference, dreams, fantasies, and free association. Patients satisfactorily relate elements of past and present relationships. As a result, patients risk giving up old behaviors no longer needed in order to adopt new behaviors.

References

Angyal, A. (1965). *Neurosis and Treatment: A Holistic Theory*. New York: Wiley.

Balint, M. (1968). *The Basic Fault: Therapeutic Aspects of Regression*. New York: Brunner/Mazel.

Bateson, G., Jackson, D., Haley, J., and Weakland, J. H. (1956). Toward a theory of schizophrenia. *Behavioral Science* 1(4):251–264.

Berne, E. (1961). *Transactional Analysis in Psychotherapy*. New York: Grove.

_____ (1974). *What Do You Say after You Say Hello?* New York: Grove.

Bettelheim, B. (1982). *Freud and Man's Soul*. New York: Alfred A. Knopf.

Bowlby, J. (1969). *Attachment and Loss*. Vol. 1: *Attachment*. New York: Basic Books.

_____ (1973). *Attachment and Loss*. Vol. 2: *Separation*. New York: Basic Books.

_____ (1980). *Attachment and Loss*. Vol. 3: *Loss*. New York: Basic Books.

Boyer, L. B., and Giovacchini, R. (1967). *Psychoanalytic Treatment of Schizophrenia, Borderline and Characterological Disorders*. New York: Jason Aronson.

Brown, J. R. (1986). *I Only Want What's Best for You*. New York: St. Martin's.

Cardinal, M. (1983). *The Words to Say It.* Cambridge, MA: VanVactor and Goodheart.

Chapman, A. H. (1978). *The Treatment Techniques of Harry Stack Sullivan.* New York: Brunner/Mazel.

Chatham, P. M. (1985). *Treatment of the Borderline Personality.* Northvale, NJ: Jason Aronson.

Chernin, K. (1985). *The Hungry Self.* New York: Harper and Row.

Crawford, C. (1978). *Mommie Dearest.* New York: Berkley Books.

Davanloo, H. (1978). *Basic Principles and Techniques in Short-term Dynamic Psychotherapy.* New York: Spectrum.

Friday, N. (1977). *My Mother, My Self.* New York: Dell.

Gardner, R. A. (1985). *Separation Anxiety Disorder: Psychodynamics and Psychotherapy.* Cresskill, NJ: Creative Therapeutics.

Giovacchini, P. (1984). *Character Disorders and Adaptive Mechanisms.* New York: Jason Aronson.

_____ (1986). *Developmental Disorders.* Northvale, NJ: Jason Aronson.

Gould, R. L. (1978). *Transformation: Growth and Change in Adult Life.* New York: Simon & Schuster.

Greben, S. E. (1984). *Love's Labor: Twenty-Five Years of Experience in the Practice of Psychotherapy.* New York: Schocken Books.

Grinker, R. R., and Werble, B. (1977). *The Borderline Patient.* New York: Jason Aronson.

Grotstein, J. S. (1981). *Splitting and Projective Identification.* New York: Jason Aronson.

Gunderson, J. G., and Singer, M. T. (1975). Defining borderline patients: an overview. *American Journal of Psychiatry* 132(1):1–10.

Halpern, H. M. (1976). *Cutting Loose: An Adult Guide to Coming to Terms with Your Parents.* New York: Bantam.

_____ (1982). *How to Break Your Addiction to a Person.* New York: Bantam.

Hedges, L. E. (1983). *Listening Perspectives in Psychotherapy.* New York: Jason Aronson.

Johnson, S. M. (1985). *Characterological Transformation: The Hard Work Miracle.* New York: Norton.

Kaiser, H. (1965). *Effective Psychotherapy.* New York: The Free Press.

Kaplan, L. J. (1978). *Oneness and Separateness: From Infant to Individual.* New York: Simon & Schuster.

Kernberg, O. (1972). Early ego integration and object relations. *Annals of the New York Academy of Science* 193:233–247.

_____ (1980). *Internal World and External Reality*. New York: Jason Aronson.

_____ (1984). *Severe Personality Disorders*. New Haven: Yale University Press.

Langs, R. (1973). *The Technique of Psychoanalytic Psychotherapy*. Vol. 1: *The Initial Contact: Theoretical Framework: Understanding the Patient's Communications: The Therapist's Interventions*. New York: Jason Aronson.

_____ (1974). *The Technique of Psychoanalytic Psychotherapy*. Vol. 2: *Responses to Interventions: The Patient–Therapist Relationship: The Phases of Psychotherapy*. New York: Jason Aronson.

Lawrence, D. H. (1913). *Sons and Lovers*. London: Duckworth & Sons.

Lerner, H. G. (1985). *The Dance of Anger*. New York: Harper & Row.

Lidz, T. (1973). *The Origin and Treatment of Schizophrenic Disorders*. New York: Basic Books.

Lindner, R. (1955). *The Fifty-Minute Hour*. New York: Jason Aronson, 1982.

MacKinnon, R. A., and Michels, R. (1971). *The Psychiatric Interview: In Clinical Practice*. Philadelphia: W. B. Saunders.

Mahler, M. (1974). Symbiosis and individuation: the psychological birth of the human infant. *The Psychoanalytic Study of the Child* 29:89–106.

_____ (1975). *The Psychological Birth of the Human Infant*. New York: Basic Books.

Mann, J. (1973). *Time-Limited Psychotherapy*. Cambridge, MA: Harvard Press.

Masterson, J. F. (1972). *Treatment of the Borderline Adolescent: A Developmental Approach*. New York: Wiley.

_____ (1976). *Psychotherapy of the Borderline Adult: A Developmental Approach*. New York: Brunner/Mazel.

_____ (1981). *The Narcissistic and Borderline Disorders: An Integrated Developmental Approach*. New York: Brunner/Mazel.

_____ (1983). *Countertransference and Psychotherapeutic Techniques: Teaching Seminars of the Psychotherapy of the Borderline Adult*. New York: Brunner/Mazel.

_____ (1985). *The Real Self: A Developmental, Self, and Object Relations Approach*. New York: Brunner/Mazel.

Masterson, J. F., and Rinsley, D. B. (1975). The borderline syndrome: the role of the mother in the genesis and psychic structure of the borderline personality. *International Journal of Psycho-Analysis* 56(2):163–177.

Miller, A. (1981). *Prisoners of Childhood: How Narcissistic Parents Form and Deform the Emotional Lives of Their Gifted Children.* New York: Basic Books.

_____ (1984). *Thou Shalt Not Be Aware: Society's Betrayal of the Child.* New York: Farrar, Straus & Giroux.

Mitchell, S. A. (1981). The origin of the nature of the "objects" in the theories of Klein and Fairbairn. *Contemporary Psychoanalysis* 17(3):374–398.

Nichols, M. (1984). *Family Therapy.* New York: Gardner.

Norwood, N. (1985). *Women Who Love Too Much.* Los Angeles: Jeremy P. Tarcher.

Ogden, T. H. (1979). On projective identification. *International Journal of Psycho-Analysis* 60:357–373.

Peck, M. S. (1978). *The Road Less Traveled.* New York: Simon & Schuster.

_____ (1983). *People of the Lie.* New York: Simon & Schuster.

Reiser, D. E., and Levenson, H. (1984). Abuses of the borderline diagnosis: a clinical problem with teaching opportunities. *American Journal of Psychiatry* 141:12.

Rinsley, D. B. (1981). Borderline psychopathology: the concepts of Masterson and Rinsley and beyond. *Adolescent Psychiatry* 9:259–274.

_____ (1982). *Borderline and Other Self Disorders.* New York: Jason Aronson.

_____ (1984). A comparison of borderline and narcissistic personality disorders. *Bulletin of the Menninger Clinic* 48(1):1–9.

_____ (1985). Notes of the pathogenesis and nosology of borderline and narcissistic personality disorders. *Journal of the American Academy of Psychoanalysis* 13(3):317–318.

Rossner, J. (1983). *August.* New York: Warner.

Sass, L. (1982). The borderline personality. *The New York Times Magazine,* August 22.

Searles, H. F. (1986). *My Work with Borderline Patients.* Northvale, NJ: Jason Aronson.

Sheehy, G. (1976). *Passages: Predictable Crises of Adult Life*. New York: E. P. Dutton.

_____ (1981). *Pathfinders*. New York: Bantam.

Slipp, S. (1984). *Object Relations: A Dynamic Bridge between Individual and Family Treatment*. New York: Jason Aronson.

Small, L. (1979). *The Briefer Psychotherapy*. New York: Brunner/Mazel.

Stone, M. (1980). *The Borderline Syndromes: Constitution, Personality and Adaptation*. New York: McGraw-Hill.

_____ (1986). *Essential Papers on Borderline Disorders*. New York: New York University Press.

Sullivan, H. S. (1956). *Clinical Studies in Psychiatry*. New York: Norton.

Taft, J. (1962). *The Dynamics of Therapy in a Controlled Relationship*. New York: Dover.

Tyler, A. (1982). *Dinner at the Homesick Restaurant*. New York: Berkley Books.

_____ (1964). *If Morning Ever Comes*. New York: Berkley Books.

Vaillant, G. E. (1977). *Adaptation to Life: How the Best and the Brightest Came of Age*. Boston: Little, Brown.

Waugh, E. (1944). *Brideshead Revisited*. Boston: Little, Brown.

Wells, M., and Glickaul, H. C. (1986). Techniques to develop object constancy with borderline clients. *Psychotherapy* 23:460–468.

Winnicott, D. W. (1958). *Through Pediatrics to Psycho–Analysis*. New York: Basic Books.

_____ (1965). *The Maturational Processes and the Facilitating Environment*. New York: International Universities Press.

Wolberg, L. R. (1980). *Short-Term Psychotherapy*. New York: Thieme-Stratton.

Wynne, L. C., Cromwell, R. L., and Matthysse, S. (1978). *The Nature of Schizophrenia*. New York: Wiley.

Wynne, L. C., Ryckoff, I., Day, J., and Hirsh, S. L. (1958). Pseudomutuality in the family relationships of schizophrenics. *Psychiatry* 21:205–220.

Yalom, I. D., and Elkin G. (1974). *Every Day Gets a Little Closer*. New York: Basic Books.

Index

PRINTED IN U.S.A.